BYZANTIUM

AN INTRODUCTION

By arrangement with the
BRITISH BROADCASTING CORPORATION

BYZANTIUM

AN INTRODUCTION

Edited by

PHILIP WHITTING

NEW YORK UNIVERSITY PRESS

NEW YORK

1971

Library of Congress Catalogue Card Number: 76–148056

SBN 8147–9152–2

Manufactured in Great Britain

Contents

		PAGE
	INTRODUCTION	ix
I	CONSTANTINE THE GREAT AND THE CHRISTIAN CAPITAL—A.D. 324–527. By C. E. Stevens	1
II	JUSTINIAN I AND HIS SUCCESSORS— A.D. 527–610. By Donald M. Nicol	15
III	HERACLIUS, THE THREATS FROM THE EAST AND ICONOCLASM—A.D. 610–843. By Cyril Mango	39
IV	THE AGE OF CONQUEST—A.D. 842–1050. By Romilly Jenkins	61
V	THE FIRST ENCOUNTER WITH THE WEST—A.D. 1050–1204. By Anthony Bryer	83
VI	THE SECOND ENCOUNTER WITH THE WEST—A.D. 1204–1453. By Joseph Gill, S.J.	111
VII	BYZANTINE ART AND ARCHITECTURE. By Philip Whitting	135
	CHRONOLOGY	164
	INDEX	173

Plates

The plate section is situated between pp. 138 and 139.
References to the text are printed in square brackets.

1a   Mosaic—*Crucifixion*: St. Luke in Stiris (Greece) [152]
1b   Mosaic—*Anastasis*: Nea Mone (Chios) [152]

2a   Mosaic—*Crucifixion*: Daphni (Greece) [152]
2b   Church of the Dormition from the NE: Daphni (Greece) [153]

3a   Mosaic—*Leo VI*: Holy Wisdom (Istanbul) narthex [140, 148, 152]
3b   Mosaic—*Deesis*: Holy Wisdom (Istanbul) gallery [156]

4a   Mosaic—*First Seven Steps of the Virgin*: Kariye Camii (Istanbul) [157]
4b   Wall Painting—*Anastasis*: Kariye Camii (Istanbul) [157]

5a   Enamels—*Crown of St. Andrew* (Buda Pest): Constantine IX—Zoe—Theodora [154]
5b   Ivory—*The Veroli Casket* (London) [153]

6a   Mosaic—*Virgin Hodegetria*: Kariye Camii (Istanbul) [147]
6b   Ivory—*Constantine VII* (Moscow) [154]

7a   Imperial Palace—*Tekfur Saray* (Istanbul) [159]
7b   Coins—(i) Alexius I [155] (ii) John II [155] (iii) Heraclius [143, 150] (iv) Justinian I [17] (v) Justinian II [150, 151] (vi) Leo III and Constantine V [45, 139, 150] (vii) Nicephorus II [77]

8a   Wall Painting—*Lamentation*: Nerezi (Yugoslavia) [138, 155–6]
8b   Mosaic—*Pantocrator*: Fetiye Camii (Istanbul) [157]

Maps and Ground Plans

facing page

1   Justinian I's Empire, *c.* 565 (based on Uspenskij,
    Istorija Vizantijskoj Imperii, Vol. 1, p. 40)   18

2   The Organization of the Themes in Asia Minor in
    the Seventh to Ninth Centuries   50

3   Basil II's Empire, *c.* 1025   66

4   The Empire under the Comneni   98

5   The Age of Latin rule in Constantinople   114

6   The Collapse of the Byzantine Empire in the
    Fourteenth Century   130

    S. Apollinare in Classe, near Ravenna   *page* 144
    S. Vitale, Ravenna   144

The designs for chapter headings were drawn from coins as follows: Chapter I—Constantine I, from a gold solidus of Nicomedia: *c.* 335; Chapter II—Justinian I, from a gold piece of 36 solidi, now lost: *c.* 534; Chapter III—Heraclius, from a gold solidus of Constantinople: *c.* 610; Chapter IV—Basil II and Constantine VIII, from a gold nomisma with Basil II on the left: *c.* 980; Chapter V—An electrum tetarteron of Alexius I, pre-Reform coinage: *c.* 1090; Chapter VI—John VIII, from a bronze medallion by Pisanello: *c.* 1438; Chapter VII—Bust of Jesus, from a gold solidus of Constantine VII: *c.* 950.

Acknowledgements

The publisher's thanks are due to the following for permission to reproduce maps and plates: Cambridge University Press for Maps 2–6; Greek Tourist Organization for Plate 1b; Josephine Powell, Rome, for Plates 1a, 2a, 4a, 8a; A. F. Kersting for Plate 2b; Hirmer Foto-archiv, München, for Plates 3b, 6b, 7a; André Held for Plate 4b; Hungarian National Museum for Plate 5a; Victoria and Albert Museum for Plate 5b; Byzantine Institute Inc. for Plates 3a, 6a; Ashmolean Museum for Plate 7b; Philip Whitting for Plate 8b. The ground plan of S. Apollinare on p. 144 is reproduced by kind permission of Longmans, from *Simpson's History of Architectural Development Vol II: Early Christian, Byzantine and Romanesque Architecture* by Cecil Stewart; and that of S. Vitale on the same page by kind permission of BBC Publications.

Introduction

In recent years there has been a significant change in the English-speaking countries, both in the attitude of the public and of scholars, to Byzantine history and art. Many books on different aspects of Byzantine art in particular, have been published and have found an enthusiastic response. This in turn has inspired a desire for more knowledge of the historical background by people whose previous experience had left the field totally unexplored. There is more interest in universities too and specialist books appear regularly, enabling new and more precise perspectives to be obtained: even in schools questions at general and advanced certificate levels can be expected. The time seems ripe for a book to help students beginning the subject and others interested in a more general way, who want to have at once an over-all view and some sure foundations on which to build. The ease of travel has opened so many of the finest monuments of the Byzantine era to a wide public that a few words of guidance as to what these are, where they are to be sought and how they can be studied, seem to be an appropriate addition.

This is, then, a book for the beginner designed to highlight some points and to simplify others in a story composite in background, long drawn out in the time-scale, often complex both as to external relations and internally, let alone still insufficiently explored by scholars. Much of it takes place in what we in the West tend to refer to as the Dark Ages. Yet it is abundantly clear that western European history, and above all its art history, need to be more closely related to Byzantine developments than they have been in the past.

The book is based on a series of programmes on Byzantine

history and Byzantine art arranged by the British Broadcasting Corporation in 1968 and broadcast in the 'Study Session'. As a background to the series, and especially to support the art discussions, the BBC produced a paperback *Byzantium*,* including some 50 illustrations. In producing the talks in book form it has been possible to expand some points and to introduce a few new ones; bibliographies have been enlarged and notes included where authors have thought it necessary. The chapter on Art and Architecture is more independent of the BBC discussions in form but includes much of the material that arose in them. However great the changes have been, acknowledgement must be made to the staff of the BBC and, in particular, to producer Adrian Johnson, who assembled a distinguished team of historians and guided their presentation with an experienced hand. His enthusiasm, along with that of G. Walton Scott, producer of the art discussions and of much of the booklet, played a big part in achieving a successful result and the work of both is reflected in this book.

One of the initial difficulties in Byzantine history is to decide on where to start. The alternatives that have been suggested and well supported are Constantine the Great† and his fixing of the capital of the Roman Empire at Byzantium, the reign of Theodosius I which witnessed the effective elimination of paganism, Justinian I with his attempted restoration of the Roman Empire in the West after the barbarian invasions, the reign of Heraclius when something very different and differently organised from the old Roman Empire had emerged, or that of Leo III the author of the Iconoclastic decrees and protagonist against the Arab invasions. These alternatives are spread over four centuries and bear witness to the complex situation in the eastern half of the old Roman Empire which

---

* Details of this booklet which is still obtainable from *BBC Publications, London W1A 1AA*, appear in the bibliography following Chapter VII.

† Reference to the Chronology on page 164 may be useful here, particularly to 330, 392, 527, 610 and 717.

had survived the first onset of barbarian invaders, until at the end of the VIth century Slavs and Avars broke through in the Balkans; at the same time on the eastern frontier the old Persian enemy after a last unsuccessful fling was replaced by the even more dangerous Muslims from the deserts of Arabia. Most people have found it more satisfactory to go back to Constantine from whose remarkable actions so much of subsequent history stems: Mr. C. E. Stevens, a well-known Oxford tutor in Ancient History therefore introduces Byzantine history here with a backward as well as a forward look which will set the stage for readers. He is followed by Dr. D. M. Nicol of the Department of History at Edinburgh University who concentrates his attention upon Justinian I who was long regarded as presiding over the first 'golden age' of Byzantium but many of whose achievements are seen to be short-lived and his objectives scarcely viable. Next Professor Cyril Mango from the Institute of Byzantine Studies at Dumbarton Oaks, deals with the reign of Heraclius and the period of Iconoclasm in a single chapter— a difficult task involving great successes, quickly changed into disaster and finally a drastic reappraisal of the situation by Leo III. Professor Romilly Jenkins, Director of Studies at Dumbarton Oaks, deals with the period of reconquest under the popular Macedonian dynasty, highlighting the conditions that brought military superiority.* But the strains involved in incessant wars proved too great for the Empire and fifty years after the death of the triumphant Macedonian Basil II, the Seljuq Turks after one major victory could raid and occupy the central highlands of Anatolia, virtually without opposition. This is where Dr. A. A. M. Bryer of the History Department in Birmingham University begins his story of 'The First Encounter with the West', as the Emperors of the family of Comnenus while stabilising the situation in the East had also to face Norman attacks in the West. Dr. Bryer shows how the Empire

---

* To the great regret of Byzantinists and friends everywhere, Professor Romilly Jenkins died in October 1969 while this book was in preparation.

disintegrated into its national parts before the Fourth Crusaders set up their short-lived Latin Empire after their conquest of Constantinople in 1204. Professor Joseph Gill, S.J., describes the last two centuries and a half of the Empire's story in Chapter VI, 'The Second Encounter with the West'. He includes the Latin Empire and the restoration of Greek rulers in the shape of the Palaeologus family, focussing attention on the major problem of the Union of the Churches, from which Western assistance might have been gained, rather than on the Turks under whose suzerainty the Emperors ruled for many years. Professor Gill is one of the very few with the knowledge and experience to provide sure guidance in a fantastically complicated as well as lengthy period. Finally there is a chapter by the editor on Byzantine Art and Architecture, considered chronologically so that it can be fitted into the historical treatment, though as explained there, it is not always easy to do this.

Each chapter has a bibliography to enable those particularly interested to pursue the subject further. It will be noticed that where suitable books are few, particularly in the chapters by Professor Mango and Professor Jenkins, authors have added notes to their text referring to original authorities and less easily obtained secondary ones. It may be useful here to draw attention to certain books readily available, which any interested reader would do well to refer to whether or not they are mentioned in the bibliographies:

Ostrogorsky, G., *History of the Byzantine State*. Oxford, Basil Black-well, 2nd edition 1968.

Hussey, J. M. (ed.), *The Cambridge Mediaeval History*, vol. IV, Parts I and II. Cambridge U.P., 2nd edition 1966 and 1967.

Vasiliev, A. A., *History of the Byzantine Empire 324–1453*. Wisconsin U.P., 1952.

Bury, J. B., *History of the Later Roman Empire 395–800*. London, Macmillan 1889 (2nd edition 395–565 in 1923).

For a lively, stimulating account of Byzantine culture, Robert Byron's *The Byzantine Achievement* (Routledge, 1929) is still fresh and valuable while Professor Norman Baynes' lecture *The Thought World of East Rome* (reprinted in *Byzantine Studies and other Essays*, London, Athlone Press, 1955) gives an unusual entry into the daily life of an age, somehow concentrating into a few pages the lifetime's work of a great scholar. Professor Baynes with H. St. L. B. Moss edited a series of more matter-of-fact essays on aspects of Byzantine history and culture in *Byzantium* (Oxford University Press, 1948), which can be very useful for quick reference.

The maps are those used in Ostrogorsky's *History of the Byzantine State* and we express our gratitude to the Cambridge University Press for permission to use No. 2–No. 6 which were originally drawn for the *Cambridge Mediaeval History*, vol. IV, Part I, referred to above. They provide a strong visual buttress to the text, conveying valuable lessons of their own as a comparison between 'Justinian's Empire' (No. 1) and 'The Collapse of the Byzantine Empire in the Fourteenth Century' (No. 6) will amply demonstrate. The illustrations have been chosen with the Art and Architecture chapter primarily in mind, but some imperial portraits have been included amongst them.

Something must be said about the rendering of Byzantine names. Customary usage, neglect and inadequate knowledge of the background, the basic difficulties of transliteration and translation, and the number of languages involved present intimidating problems to everyone handling the subject. Is it to be Alexius or Alexios, Amorium or Amorion, Phokas, Phocas or (as on his coins) Focas, Ottoman or Osmanli, Seljuk, Seljuq or (as the Turks write it today) Selçuk? Each writer will have his preferences in inconsistency and it is in the ordinary names that most difficulty arises. The editor has sought to follow customary usage where it is not misleading and this involves generally choosing Latin in preference to Greek forms. When in doubt he follows Professor Hussey's translation of Ostrogorsky's *History* as—it cannot be repeated too often—this is a book that all interested people should be referring to. One quirk of his own the editor has followed throughout: common usage refers to the famous church in Istanbul as Saint Sophia or Sancta Sophia, sometimes Hagia Sophia with many variants: the Turks call it Aya Sofya, but here it will always be found as the Church of the Holy Wisdom. This English translation cuts through a multitude of names and avoids any connection with the IInd-century martyr whose children Faith, Hope and Charity died with her. The 'Holy Wisdom' is that of the New Testament and the dedication is therefore to Jesus himself. It will be noticed that when the church became a mosque in 1453, there was no change in dedication. As readers will appreciate much is involved in the mere rendering of a name.

Although this is a book intended for those taking their first steps in the subject, some very eminent exponents of Byzantine history have agreed to contribute and the editor has felt it a great privilege to work with them. Not all of them agree on every point, but this need not trouble, and may not even be noticed by, the public that, it is hoped, will enjoy their work. On matters such as Iconoclasm, the development of feudalism and the origins of different strands in the artistic tradition, research is actively in progress, more actively than ever before. There is still room for different views and this book will perhaps be a means for a much wider circle comprehending new results as they are published, and tying them into the skeleton structure here raised for beginners.

Philip Whitting

December 1970

I

Constantine the Great and the Christian Capital, A.D. 324-527

C. E. STEVENS

In writing about the 'Byzantine Empire' we are using an odd word which may lead us astray, and we had better get the picture right at once. After 363 there were more or less continually two rulers of the Roman Empire, one in the west who was occasionally in Rome, the other in the east who was nearly always in Constantinople. The empire was still regarded as one. A decree, whether to alter the rules of intestate succession or to persecute a group of heretics, which was issued in one half was normally accepted automatically in the other, and a man might move from one to the other as he climbed the promotion ladder: the last governor of Britain whom we know, Chrysanthus, had started his career in Constantinople. But the fact of separation is underlined by the 'almanac', as we may call it, of the civil and military establishments of the Empire in the fifth century, the *Notitia Dignitatum*. It is in two volumes, one for the 'Eastern', the other for the 'Western Part'. In 476 the last remains of the 'Western Part' disappeared, but the 'Eastern Part' went on. Its historians spoke about the Romans, its population called themselves Romans and their language Romaic, though it was actually modern Greek. Romaic they called it until an independent Greece appeared. Byron writing his love-poem to a Romaic 'Maid of Athens' with the modern Greek refrain—Zoe mou sas agapo—illustrates this very neatly.

Our volume, therefore, is studying that part of the Roman Empire that survived in the east with its capital at Constantinople, and which is known as the 'Byzantine Empire' because Constantinople was first called Byzantium. It is an odd name, for Byzantium, though a very old town, played no great part in history until it did become Constantinople. Antiquarian

B

writers in Constantinople might call its subjects 'Byzantines' in contexts when 'Romans' or 'Constantinopolitans' might each be in their way confusing. The west took over the word, often with overtones of denigration, and moderns have used it (the earliest quotation in the Oxford English Dictionary is from the eighteenth century) as a convenience. But it is something of a misnomer—and somewhat misleading.

This 'Byzantine Empire' had a long life—until 1453. Strange thought, indeed, that in 476 it had nearly as long to live as all Roman history from the year when the Kings were expelled by L. Junius Brutus in 509 B.C. A Roman Emperor—Manuel II—visited England in 1400, and Gibbon picked up what his secretary thought about the Londoners: 'In the habits of their domestic life, they are not easily distinguished from their neighbours of France; but the most singular circumstance of their manners is their disregard of conjugal honour and female chastity. In their mutual visits, as the first act of hospitality, the guest is welcomed in the embraces of their wives and daughters; among friends, they are lent and borrowed without shame; nor are the islanders offended at this strange commerce and its inevitable consequences.' London, a 'swinging city'—in 1400!

There was an earlier connexion. Not only had Harold Hardrada done a stint in the Varangian, the Scandinavian, imperial bodyguard, but his conquerors at Stamford Bridge, conquered in their turn at Hastings, pressed into the guard in such numbers that, we are told, the emperor was saluted as Augustus—in the English language. Perhaps these Anglo-Saxon refugees strummed that 'Byzantine' improvement of the lyre, the *Pandiorion*. Catalans, who occupied Greece for a time (giving Shakespeare a 'Duke of Athens' for his *Midsummer Night's Dream*), took the instrument and its name to Spain, whence they were taken to the West Indies by Columbus and his fellows, only to return to us as the Banjo. Truly this 'Byzantine Empire' lasted a long time with some very odd fruits. One asks oneself in the idiom of today: 'What made it tick?'

Gibbon does not help us to answer. The eighteenth-century

rationalist who said that he had 'described the triumph of
barbarism and religion' could only speak with malevolence of
an institution which was based firmly and squarely on the
latter. He introduced the single chapter which he thought
adequate for five hundred years of Byzantine political history
with the full blasts of scorn. One sentence will give the measure
of it: 'The subjects of the Byzantine empire, who assume and
dishonour the names both of Greeks and Romans, present a
dead uniformity of abject vices, which are neither softened by
the weakness of humanity nor animated by the vigour of memorable crimes.' And we have accepted his values. We are ex-
horted to die like the Spartans of Thermopylae, we do it 'in the
high Roman fashion'. But our bureaucracy 'whose worm dieth
not' is Byzantine.

It was quite unfair, and we can refute it from Gibbon himself. The Byzantine Empire has an amazing collection of heroic
figures. We can start with Belisarius, and there is the strange,
erratic Heraclius. Great names follow: Leo III, who repulsed
the Saracens from Constantinople; John Zimisces, victorious
from the Danube to the Taurus; Basil II, 'Slayer of Bulgarians';
the almost legendary exploits of the Comneni—all to be found
in Gibbon's own pages—and these are only the first flighters.
And these men had foes worthy of their steel.

Public men (and they include historians) of an aristocratic
age could see themselves as the spiritual offspring of the Roman
senators who wore down Hannibal to defeat because they
would not 'despair of the republic'. They forgot that Roman
armies of the great days were often defeated by barbarians,
though one of their generals almost anticipated Hilaire Belloc
on British victories over 'natives' when he told his troops:

> The happy thing is we have got
> The—breastplate and the helmet—and they have not.

The enemies of our Byzantines had both—and two other
things quite unknown to the foes of Caesar and Pompey—
religious fanaticism and the stirrup. Yet the Byzantines

'managed' the Huns, they held the Slavs at arm's length, they grappled with the Arabs and saw their fanaticism fretted away by luxury. Then it was the Seljuq Turks—more fanatical horse-men—and the Byzantines fought them hard. It can, in fact, be argued that it was the 'Crime of 1204' that delivered Constan-tinople—250 years later—to the Ottomans, with Constantine Palaeologus dying, like a Spartan of Thermopylae, in the breach. There is the art that we are learning to admire more and more; there is, if one looks at it fairly, the best historical writing that the Greek lands produced since Polybius in the second century B.C.; and they gave the world an inter-national currency, so to say, in their stride. And all this when the west was something like a shambles. How on earth did they do it? This chapter hopes, at least, to make the answer easier by showing how Constantine the Great and his succes-sors built the stage on which they could play their parts.

The emperor Diocletian (284–305) had thought to take the Roman Empire out of the chaos of the third century by turning its government into something like a family firm: two senior and two junior partners, with the juniors in due course becom-ing seniors and creating from the results of marriage alliances two fresh juniors—and so into the future. The scheme crashed at once; and Constantine, the son of Constantius, a junior elevated to 'seniority' who died soon after at York in 306, was an agent of its crashing. With the defeat of Licinius, ruler of the east, in 324, Constantine was master of the whole Roman Empire. It sounds like the mere successful militarism of a South American general, but it was much more.

Constantine is one of those world figures who defy historians just because they are so unlike them, men with an insight that they cannot themselves define, that perhaps they do not even know in their conscious selves. A man who recalls great cap-tains of industry, a Ford, a Nuffield, recalls great poets too, a Blake, a Coleridge, a man not at all like a great historian, cool-headed in his library. Constantine gave the Roman Empire a new capital city by turning Byzantium into Constantinople;

he gave it a new state religion by adopting Christianity as his own. And he took the decisive steps to both in 324. Where does the calculation of a statesman end and the insight of a poet begin with this uneducated soldier who could not speak to Greek bishops in their own language? The historians cannot answer.

Ever since it existed at all, the Roman Empire was more of a juxtaposition than an amalgam of two dominant societies, the Roman and the Greek. Romans despised Greeks for lack of character, Greeks despised Romans for lack of culture—neither, of course, fairly. But in Constantine's time the Greeks had a case; for Roman literature, though not far from a period of revival, was almost dead, while Greek intellectuals were very active indeed. Much of their activity reads to us either as shallow or as mystically nonsensical. But the activity was there. The 'Eastern Part' deserved to have the capital of a united empire and would need one if it split—and we can credit Constantine with a notion that a split was likely.

In a way a split was part of Diocletian's scheme. He had chosen the east as his 'sphere of influence' and operated his rule from the base of Nicomedia, an attractive town near Byzantium on the Asiatic side. But Nicomedia had been the place where the edicts of Christian persecution had been issued. Constantine was not going to pick on Nicomedia.

In fact, Byzantium was a much better choice. With command of the sea, it could be, and fifth-century improvements ensured that it was, an impregnable fortress (command of the sea was lost in 1204 and 1453). It was well placed for two danger areas, the Danube and the eastern frontier; and, with command of the Dardanelles, the two dangers could be insulated. And it was going to become a great entrepôt of world trade. Historians have doubted whether Constantine was thinking of any of these things. But Constantine is a man to baffle the historians.

The year when he started rebuilding Constantinople was the year when he summoned the first Ecumenical Council of the Church, the Council of Nicaea, over which he acted as presiding officer. In his opening speech, Constantine explained that he looked forward to a day when (by persuasion rather than persecution) his whole empire would accept the Christian revelation; and he said (as he was always saying) that Christianity was the right religion because the Christian God had produced for him the 'miracles' which had led him in a kind of *via sacra* from Britain to the east. It followed that if all his subjects were Christians, the empire must prosper. He was disappointed rather than disillusioned to discover that Christians might differ on what Christianity was.

Historians have often remarked that Constantine's Christianity was very much a shot in the dark. When he proclaimed his adherence to it, less than ten per cent of the Roman Empire was Christian, and a politically unimportant ten per cent at that. Did he have an insight into the 'historical necessity' of an œcumenical religion for an œcumenical empire, an insight into medieval doctrines (inspiring Dante) of Emperor and Pope? Again Constantine baffles the historians.

We can see him drawing the traditional trench round the projected site, we can hear his words in the language of Gibbon: 'On foot, with a lance in hand, the emperor himself led the solemn procession, and directed the line, which was traced as the boundary of the destined capital, till the growing circumference was observed with astonishment by the assistants, who at length ventured to observe that he had already exceeded the most ample measure of a great city. 'I shall still advance,' replied Constantine, 'till HE, the invisible guide who marches before me, thinks proper to stop.' He ensured that Constantinople would be a populous city: it soon had a quarter of a million inhabitants (with 10,000 beggars). It was not quite a 'clean' Christian town, but it was a town in which churches vastly outnumbered temples. A town where men discussed Christianity as they might now discuss the prospects of the local football team. As Gregory, Bishop of Nyssa, put it when visiting Constantinople about 370 (the translation again is Gibbon's): 'If you desire a man to change a piece of silver, he

informs you wherein the Son differs from the Father; if you
ask the price of a loaf, you are told by way of reply that the
Son is inferior to the Father; and if you inquire whether the
bath is ready, the answer is that the Son was made out of
nothing.' The impregnable capital of a state with a state
religion. A picture begins to emerge.

The successors of Constantine, ruling at his Constantinople
are, if we except the meteoric career (361–363) of Julian the
Apostate who hoped to put back the clock if pagans, with their
multifarious cults, could be persuaded that they were Platonic
philosophers if only they knew it, a dull set. It is no accident
that the dullest chapter of the *Cambridge Medieval History*, not
conspicuous for excitement, should deal with them. Their problems, however, were concerned with Constantine's two-pronged
action of 324, the impregnable capital and the state religion
of Christianity—the problems, in fact, of barbarians outside the
empire and heretics within it. And with both we can say that
they lost the battles, but won the war.

Forty years after Constantine's death, some crisis in central
Asia (climatologists have suspected a sudden desiccation) set
the terrible Huns on the move; and the horrified descriptions
which contemporaries give of them suggest a Martian invasion
in science fiction. Their advance produced that 'Wandering of
the Nations' which brought Vandals from the Baltic to Africa,
Franks and Burgundians of West Germany to France—and
Hengist and Horsa to England.

The 'Eastern Part' felt it first. Under pressure from Huns
the Goths as a body requested to be taken into the empire across
the Danube; and the Roman immigration officers were both
incompetent and avaricious. The barbarians revolted and inflicted on the army of the 'Eastern Part' the worst defeat that
Roman arms had suffered for more than five hundred years. At
the Battle of Adrianople (378), the Roman Army of the Danube
simply disappeared. What mattered in the next thirty years was
what this or that barbarian chief was thinking and what he
might do. They were saying at this time in Vienne—'Nothing

is done at the Gallic court without the consent of Franks.' With the Goths under Gainas and Tribigild around, the same thing could be said at Constantinople. The ultimate problem was, in the most literal sense of the words, to get the barbarians where one wanted them, until the patterns of defence—and an army to conduct it—could be re-created; and the statesmen of the fifth century solved it—after a fashion. The immediate problem was to get them out of Constantinople, to make the city impregnable—for Constantinopolitans. And it was solved by one of those dramatic strokes which repeat themselves in different contexts all through Byzantine history. The year is 400, the narrator Bishop Synesius.

The Gothic 'army of occupation' was partly in Constantinople and partly outside it, and Gainas, its commander, was operating a change-over—at dawn to avoid disturbances. As the troops going out with all their baggage (including loot from the citizens) approached a gate, they passed an old beggar woman, who screamed rude remarks about barbarians. A Goth raised his sword to strike her down. A rescuer appeared, and soon there was a riot between the mob and the 'army of occupation' within. The mob shut the gates and the army without lost its nerve and retreated. The army within was cornered and cut down in an orgy of street fighting.

It was an accident, and accidents, as historians know, do not turn world history. But, as they know too, there are accidents which are accidentally significant; and of this kind is the accident of the beggar woman at the gate. The year 400 was not the end of the barbarian commanders at the court of the emperor, but it was the end of barbarian warriors within the walls. Constantinople was master in its own house.

The next problem for statesmen was the Huns. Under Attila they were able to dominate all the Germanic north. But the policy makers at Constantinople may well have realised (our sources are too poor for us to assert that they did) that Attila's empire rested on the personality of Attila alone, and that it was worth buying time and paying a high price for it. The

impregnable city and the control of the Dardanelles yielded
their dividend: the unapproachable province of Asia Minor
could raise the cash to pay the tribute that Attila demanded. In
451 he turned westwards to meet defeat on the 'Plains of
Chalons'. Two years later he was dead and his empire gone
with the wind. The emperors of the 'Eastern Part' had lost
Adrianople and quite a few other battles, but they had, in a
manner, won the war. For the verdict was given for the
future. There would be no Genseric the Vandal at Constantinople, no Clovis the Frank—no Hengist and Horsa. We can
feel the contrast in literature, as Dr Frend gives it to us. To the
great churchmen of the west in the fifth century, to Augustine
and Salvian of Marseilles, 'the father of sociology', the world
is hopelessly evil and man must await in passivity his salvation
in heaven. But for the two historians of the church in the east,
Socrates and Sozomen, there is hope, there is even cheerfulness.
The road of Augustine and Salvian leads to 476, the road of
Socrates and Sozomen—to the 'Byzantine Empire'.

Socrates finished his history in 429 with a confidence in the
future of the Church. But this was a very bad shot. If the problem of the barbarians outside was moving towards a hopeful
solution, the problem of heresy within was about to start.

Constantine's disappointments in 324 were especially aroused
by disputes of the Arian faction about the relationship of the
Father and the Son (we remember in this context the banker,
the baker and the bath-attendant!); but Theodosius had virtually persecuted it out of existence at the end of the fourth century (though not among converted barbarians, which is another
story). In the next century, however, a much more pertinacious
dispute arose, on the right mixture of the Human and the
Divine in the Person of Jesus Christ. The Nestorians laid stress
on the Human, but were soon eliminated, surviving only—to
this day—as a refugee minority in Mesopotamia outside the
empire; the Monophysites laid stress on the Divine. The serious
theological battles were between them and the Orthodox, who
kept—and keep—that middle position defined in the Athana-

sian Creed as 'neither dividing the persons nor confounding the substance'.

These battles were far more dangerous politically than the Arian disputes because provincial loyalties were beginning to express themselves in religious sectarianism. It is a little like the varieties of 'communism' today. The south-eastern parts of the Constantinople Empire—Syria, Palestine and Egypt—tended to be Monophysite, Asia Minor and the Balkans Orthodox, while the Pope with the west behind him was unswervingly Orthodox too. Three Œcumenical Councils set the stage of theological warfare. Ephesus I in 431 (so much for the optimism of Socrates!) condemned Nestorius, though it was Cyril, patriarch of Alexandria, a near-Monophysite, who delivered the *coup de grâce*. Ephesus II in 449 gave victory to the Monophysites (and was hence for the Pope the 'Brigands' Council'), but Orthodoxy won in 451 at Chalcedon. The emperor in Constantinople was in a perpetual dilemma. If he favoured Monophysites, he would keep the 'south-east', could intimidate the patriarch on the spot and through him hope to keep something of Asia Minor and the Balkans; but he would certainly lose the Pope and the west. If he moved towards the Pope's position, there was a certainty of hostility from the 'south-east'. Theologians, including Justinian, searched for a formula which would evade the dilemma, but they never found one.

In fact, Justinian, with his eyes on the great plan of reconquest in the west, came down with some hesitation (Theodora had other views) on the side of Orthodoxy, and his formula was a hopeful gesture to the 'south-east' which the 'south-east' would not have. Indeed, an Orthodox government at Constantinople would pass for 'colonialist' at Alexandria; and the Monophysite historian, Zachariah of Mytilene, can write of Roman troops intervening in an Alexandrian riot as though they were Germans in an occupied country. It is not surprising, therefore, that it was Syria, Palestine and Egypt that fell in the seventh century like ripe fruit to the Moslem invaders.

It was not so huge a disaster for Constantinople to lose them.

Again the battles were lost, but the war, in a sense, was won. For what was left was a compact and viable political unit, something like the New Turkey of Kemal with old Turkey-in-Europe and Greece added. Its administration was centralised, perhaps overcentralised, in Constantinople which dwarfs all other towns, the Vienna, one might call it, of the Byzantine Empire. Doctrinal argument did not cease ('We Greeks think,' said the patriarch of Constantinople to a visiting western prelate, Liutprand of Cremona, who grumbled because people in his own church did not) but doctrinal warfare inside the state was virtually over. Socrates was right after all, simply two hundred years too early. The Imperial Church, that could evoke more courageous fanaticism than Gibbon would admit—and the impregnable capital: truly Constantine's 'Wisdom' (the plan of the first Church of the Holy Wisdom is his) was justified of her—very remote—children. We can call him in truth the creator of the 'Byzantine Empire'. But the baker and the beggar-woman can stand beside him.

BIBLIOGRAPHY

Gibbon's *Decline and Fall* will always be the gateway to the Byzantine World for English-speaking readers. But he disliked it and was bored by it: and he was beginning to get bored with 'Eastern Rome' before Justinian (who roused him). Still there are magnificent pictures of Constantinople and of nomadic peoples (to illustrate Attila and the Huns) —and he knew neither at first hand; and the great personalities, Constantine, Julian, Athanasius, get the full treatment from his pen. The standard text with amending footnotes and appendices is edited by J. B. Bury (Methuen 1896 and many later editions). The 'Best of Gibbon' has been abridged into one volume by D. M. Low. Bury himself starts his two volume *History of the Later Roman Empire* in 395 and goes down to Justinian (London, Macmillan, 1923: 2nd edition).

For the administrative, social and economic background there is *The Later Roman Empire, 284–602* (Oxford, Basil Blackwell, 1964) by A. H. M. Jones, who read for it, as he told me, 'every word written by anyone during it which is preserved to us—except liturgical writers' and he knows how to display his wealth. It is in three volumes with a folder of maps. Professor Jones has also written a most attractive and scholarly short life of Constantine entitled *Constantine and the conversion of Europe* (London, E.U.P.—Teach Yourself History Series—1949). The best short introduction to this period is, in my opinion, *The Birth of the Middle Ages* (Oxford U.P., 1935: paperback 1963) by H. St. L. B. Moss.

The 'classic' account of Constantine with a full treatment of sources is by N. H. Baynes *Constantine the Great and the Christian Church* in *Proceedings of the British Academy* vol. 15, 1929. E. A. Thomson has an excellent study on *The History of Attila and the Huns* (Oxford U.P., 1948). Some interesting Constantinian studies are contained in *Dumbarton Oaks Papers* No. 21 (Washington: 1967).

Otherwise, very detailed studies are either very technical or (with biographies of great ecclesiastical personalities) showing a tendency to the pietistic. Exceptions are *St John Chrysostom, His Life and Times* by W. R. W. Stephens though written as long ago as 1883, and *Augustine of Hippo* by P. Brown (London, Faber, 1967).

A 'small' (and much more amusing) ecclesiastic is Synesius of Cyrene whose *Letters* have been translated and annotated by A. Fitzgerald (Oxford U.P., 1926). There is also much instruction and amusement to be had from the *Autobiography* of the principal pagan thinker, Libanius of Antioch; it has been translated by A. F. Norman (Oxford U.P., 1965). Professor A. Momigliano has edited an interesting and wide-ranging series of essays on *The Conflict between Paganism and Christianity in the Fourth Century* (Oxford, The Clarendon Press, 1963).

II

Justinian I and his Successors, A.D. 527-610
DONALD M. NICOL

The rulers of the Roman Empire, holding absolute authority over so large a part of the world, were sometimes able to shape the destiny of a whole generation or an age. The age of Justinian covered most of the sixth century. Some have called it the last century of the Roman Empire. For it was Justinian who made the last successful attempt to reunite under the rule of one man all the provinces of ancient Rome, to reconstitute the undivided and universal Empire of Augustus and the Caesars.

In the century before, most of the western part of that Empire had been lost. The Ostrogoths had established a kingdom in Italy, the Visigoths in Spain, and the Vandals in North Africa. On the eastern frontier lay the Sassanid Empire of the Persians, a greater rival to the power of Rome than any barbarian kingdom. But the Persians were a perennial and familiar problem; and the land that they occupied had never been Roman. To Justinian, and to many of his contemporaries, it was the recovery of the lost western provinces which was the obvious duty of a true Roman Emperor. And most of his reign was directed to this end.

Justinian succeeded his uncle Justin I in 527. He was already forty-five and his views on imperial policy were formed. His appearance is plain for all to see in the mosaic portraits of him in the churches at Ravenna, or in the magnificent gold and copper coins of his reign. But his character has been for ever distorted by the poison pen of the great Greek historian of the age, Procopius of Caesarea. Procopius composed a history of Justinian's wars against the Vandals, Goths and Persians, and also a flattering account of the Emperor's building works. But,

for reasons best known to himself, and strictly for private con-
sumption, he also wrote a Secret History, in which Justinian
and his wife, the famous Theodora, are lampooned as mon-
sters of wickedness and deceit. Reading between the lines of
Procopius, however, one can discern in Justinian a man strong-
willed when fortune favoured him, though hesitant in time of
crisis; a religious fanatic but with some of the qualities of a
monk; a restless person and yet a tireless, dedicated ruler. Even
Procopius admired the Emperor's ascetic nature, misdirected
though his mortifications might be. These are his words:

'As a general rule he cared little for sleep, and never over-
indulged in food or drink, but picked at the food with his
fingers before going away. For he regarded such things as a
kind of irrelevancy necessitated by nature. He would often fast
for two days and nights at a time, especially during Lent, or
live on wild herbs and water. He would sleep for not more
than an hour and then spend the rest of the night pacing up
and down. For he made it his business to be constantly vigilant,
suffering and striving for the sole purpose of bringing a continuous, daily sequence of disasters upon his subjects.'

Theodora, the belly-dancer whom Justinian defied conven-
tion to marry, fares even worse at the hands of Procopius. But
it is clear that she was possessed of no ordinary beauty, charm
and intelligence. She was a born actress and enjoyed being the
centre of attraction as the great lady of the imperial court; and
in contrast to her austere husband she revelled in the luxury,
pomp and elegance of life in the Great Palace at Constantinople. She shared to the full his conception of the majesty of
the Roman Empire. But whereas Justinian belonged to the
Latin world and thought like a Roman, Theodora was a Greek
or perhaps one may say a Byzantine. Their views on many
subjects differed. But as man and wife they complemented one
another. Justinian was devoted to her, and her death in 548
marked a turning-point in his career.

The age of Justinian was called into being by a number of

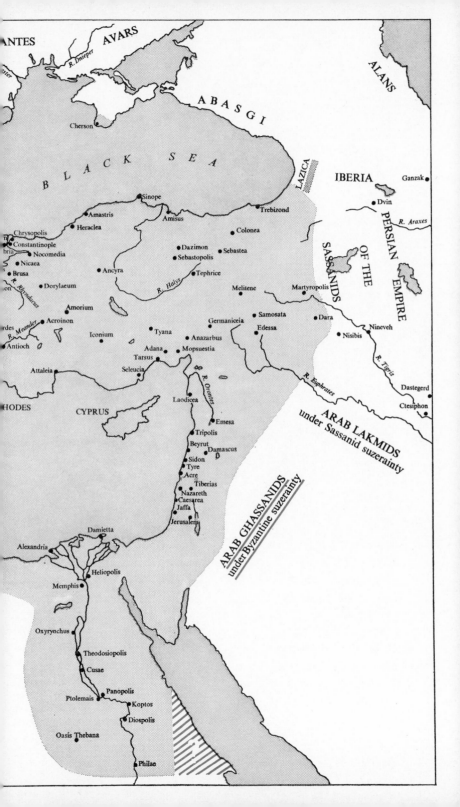

variously gifted men, who translated the Emperor's dreams into reality. There was the administrator John of Cappadocia, who became Prefect of the City, a man utterly without scruples and deservedly hated, not least by Theodora, who finally secured his disgrace. It was he who raised the taxes to pay for Justinian's ambitious schemes. There was Tribonian the lawyer, the main author of the great compilation of Roman law that Justinian commissioned. There were the generals Belisarius and Narses, fighting on all the frontiers from Syria to Italy. There were the scientists Anthemius of Tralles and Isidore of Miletus, the architects of the church of the Holy Wisdom. But the greatness of the age of itself inspired creative activity of all kinds, in poetry, painting, theology, science, medicine and the writing of history. Agathias continued the history of Procopius, but also wrote poetry and published a well-known Anthology. Romanus Melodus set the standard of Byzantine hymn-writing for the future; and a merchant seaman called Cosmas Indicopleustes related his travels to the shape and structure of the universe as he conceived it.

The inhabited part of that structure was the œcumenical or universal Christian Roman Empire whose citizens obeyed one law and professed one creed. This was the ideal before Justinian's mind. He had a passion for imposing uniformity on his heterogeneous subjects whether they wished it or not. For he was convinced that he, better than they, knew God's plan for the order of the world and was indeed God's agent for the fulfilment of that plan. Those of his subjects in Constantinople who opposed his autocratic policy were taught a bitter lesson early in his reign. The opposition showed itself in a riot that broke out in the Hippodrome in 532. Much of the city was burnt by the mob, and some of the senators proclaimed a rival Emperor. Justinian lost his nerve and would have run away, had not Theodora shamed him into action. The imperial troops were turned on the rioters, and 30,000 people were massacred in the Hippodrome.

The 'Nika riot', as it is called, was the crisis of Justinian's

C

career. Thereafter he was not troubled by political opponents. In the same year 532, after five years of border warfare, he made a treaty of peace with the king of the Persians. Many of the troops engaged on holding the eastern frontier could now be redeployed for the rescue of the western provinces. It is tempting to picture Justinian as the master-mind directing a well-planned campaign of reconquest from his headquarters in Constantinople. But in fact the work was done piece-meal, as the opportunities presented themselves. It began with the recovery of North Africa from the Vandals. Belisarius commanded the armada that set out in June 533. It was blessed by the Patriarch of Constantinople, for this was a just and holy war to liberate a Roman province from the oppression of an alien tyrant who was also, and this was worse, a heretic. The Vandal kingdom was destroyed within the year; its king Gelimer surrendered in March 534. Guerrilla warfare went on in North Africa for another fifteen years, but it was against the Berber natives and not against usurping aliens. For a lost province of the Empire had been restored to Roman rule.

The opportunity to intervene in Sicily and Italy arose in 535 when the Gothic queen Amalasuntha was murdered by her cousin Theodahad. Amalasuntha had been the friend and ally of the Roman Empire. But the Goths, like the Vandals, were Arian heretics. The salvation of the souls of the Italians, as well as their political welfare, demanded their liberation from Gothic rule. Once again the commander of the enterprise was Belisarius. In June 535 he took a fleet to Sicily, while an army marched overland into Dalmatia. Sicily fell within a few months, and on the last day of the year Belisarius entered Syracuse.

It really seemed as if divine favour smiled on Justinian's armies. In 536 he prefaced one of his edicts with these words:

'God has granted us to bring the Persians to make peace, to overthrow the Vandals, the Alans and the Moors, and to win back the whole of Africa and Sicily; and we are confident that the Lord will now grant us the power to recover the rest of our

Empire, which the Romans of earlier days extended up to the limits of the two oceans, and which they lost through their indifference.'

In a series of brilliant campaigns over the next four years Belisarius overran Italy from Naples and Rome to Ravenna. The fall of Ravenna and the capture of the Gothic king in 540 seemed to complete the operation. This was Justinian's moment of glory. But the illusion was soon shattered. In the same year the Persians broke their treaty, invaded Syria and destroyed the great city of Antioch. Belisarius had to be rushed to the eastern frontier. The Goths in Italy, who were in touch with the Persian king, then rose in rebellion. Inspired and led by Totila they soon confined the restored Roman administration to Ravenna and the southern extremities of the country. Justinian had to choose between driving the Persians out of Syria or driving the Goths out of Italy. Characteristically he tried to get the best of both worlds. Belisarius was sent back to Italy, but with a woefully inadequate army; and in 545 a truce was arranged with the Persians.

The second reconquest of Italy was a longer and bloodier affair than the first. Totila occupied Rome in 546. Belisarius managed to recover the city for a while; but in 549 he was relieved of his command. Not until 552 was the issue decided, when Narses, leading the largest army ever to take the field in Justinian's reign, met Totila and the Goths in battle at Busta Gallorum, on the road from Ravenna to Rome. By 555 the last resistance had been crushed and the Gothic régime in Italy and Sicily was at an end. It left few traces. The Goths had no appreciable effect on the racial composition or the language of the Italians. But their defeat had cost the Empire twenty years of fighting; and the expense in human suffering and devastation was incalculable. Justinian was not one to count the cost. For the fulfilment of God's plan the resources of his Empire could always be stretched a little further. In 550, when the situation in Italy was far from hopeful, he found a pretext for invading the Visigothic kingdom of Spain. A fleet was sent from Sicily, and by 551 a section of the Spanish peninsula had been conquered and reconstituted as a Roman province.

So by 555 Justinian could boast that the Mediterranean was once again a Roman lake. In the reconquered territories the old Roman provincial administration was reimposed as though there had been no change in circumstances. Sicily was placed under the rule of a praetor. Sardinia and Corsica came under the viceroy of North Africa. Italy was reconstituted as a province, governed by a Prefect with his headquarters at Ravenna; and an inscription set into a bridge over the Anio river proclaimed to the bewildered Romans that their former happiness had now been restored to them.

To many in the West, who had come to regard the Gothic régime as permanent and now found it swept away by the horrors of a war of liberation, the imperial propaganda from faraway Constantinople must have sounded hollow. In the eastern provinces, however, things were different. For until the recent invasion of Syria by the Persians the great cities of the eastern Mediterranean had continued to enjoy the security, if not the happiness, provided by the Roman Empire. Their inhabitants had not been required to adjust themselves to the collapse of their world and to the indignities of a non-Roman régime. They were accustomed to prosperity and to a high standard of living. The wealthy and sophisticated aristocracy of Constantinople expected to be provided with a steady flow of luxury goods from the far east; and Justinian did not disappoint them. The normal trade routes to India and China ran along the caravan trails through Persia, or by sea through the Indian Ocean. But the Persian Wars interrupted this traffic. Justinian therefore explored the alternative routes, by way of the Red Sea and overland by way of the Crimea, where Greek merchants already had well-established markets. But neither alternative was wholly satisfactory. The problem was partly solved when two monks, who had lived in China and there learnt the art of the manufacture of silk, were persuaded to smuggle some silk worms' eggs to Constantinople. Thenceforth, though it took many years to develop, the silk industry became one of the most flourishing and lucrative state monopolies in the Byzantine Empire.

The hope that the world had returned to the old order of the Roman Empire was fostered by Justinian's revision of the imperial laws. The Codex Justinianus, compiled by Tribonian and a legal commission in 529, contained all the valid edicts of the Emperors since the time of Hadrian, collated and arranged in orderly fashion. This was supplemented in 533 by an edition of the rulings and precedents of classical Roman lawyers called the Digest or Pandects; and in the same year a handbook for law students was published called the Institutes. The whole of this Corpus of Civil Law was written in Latin, the native language of Justinian and still the official language of the Empire. But it is significant that most of the new laws or Novels appended to it were phrased in Greek, the spoken language of the majority of the citizens in the eastern part of the Empire. For this was not simply a lawyers' collection of the imperial ordinances of ancient Rome, harking back to the past. It was an adaptation to meet the needs of a Christian state and society in the present and for the future; and even Justinian had to admit that the Greek language was fast superseding Latin as the general means of communication in the most flourishing portion of his Empire. In one of his Novels he declared: 'We have composed this decree not in the native language but in the spoken tongue of Greek, so that it may be rendered more easily intelligible to all.'

Succeeding emperors such as Leo III and Leo VI produced new legal codes to meet the changing requirements of society. But the Codex of Justinian formed the basis of all law and order in the Byzantine Empire until the fifteenth century. The Slav peoples within and beyond the imperial frontiers in due course adapted it to their own purposes; and its rediscovery by the lawyers of Bologna and the German Emperor Frederick Barbarossa in the twelfth century had profound repercussions on the development of the imperial idea in western Europe. For

Justinian's law laid great emphasis on the autocratic power of the Emperor and left little room for doubt about the legal foundation of imperial authority over the Church as well as the State.

Justinian would like to have been remembered as the restorer of the Roman Empire. But his codification of the law was a more lasting memorial than all his military conquests. His other enduring monument is the great church of the Holy Wisdom in Constantinople. Justinian built fortifications, castles and churches in almost all the provinces of his Empire. In Constantinople, however, the destruction caused by the Nika riot in 532 gave him the chance to replan and rebuild much of the city. Huge underground reservoirs, two of which survive to this day, were constructed to improve the water supply. The Great Palace of the Emperor was enlarged. New public baths, assembly halls, arcades and squares were erected, as well as a hospital and other charitable institutions; and the forum beside the Palace and the Hippodrome was adorned with a column topped by an equestrian statue of the Emperor himself. But the talents of his artists and architects were especially employed on the building or rebuilding of churches. From the monastery of St. Catherine on Mount Sinai to the churches of Ravenna in Italy Justinian's Orthodox piety was advertised. But Constantinople, the capital city of the Christian world, had to be graced and glorified with temples of exceptional magnificence. Many of the city churches were renovated; but the cathedral of the Holy Wisdom or St. Sophia was conceived and constructed on a much vaster scale, to be the new temple of the imperial faith in the New Jerusalem. There had been nothing like it before; and, though it became the model and the inspiration for generations of Byzantine and later of Muslim architects, there was nothing to equal it in the future. The architects, Anthemius of Tralles and Isidore of Miletus, were both from the eastern part of the Empire and not hide-bound by the traditions of Roman architecture. Their achievement was to enclose an immense and open space beneath an aerial dome 100 feet in diameter rising,

without visible means of support, to a height of 180 feet from
the ground. The whole building stood, and stands, as Procopius
says, like a watchtower guarding the city; and its interior,
lavishly decorated with mosaics, coloured marble, gold, silver
and ivory, presented a general effect not of religious gloom but
of spaciousness and light. The great dome seemed to Procopius
to float in the air; and the forty windows round its circumference invited the sunlight to stream through and make its home
within. Justinian is said to have boasted that he had outdone
Solomon when he first entered the church in December 537.
But the original design, executed in a mere five years, had to
be modified when the dome collapsed in 558. The reconstruction, completed in 562, was celebrated by a long poem describ-
ing the wonders of the building composed by the court poet
Paul the Silentiary.

The Church of the Holy Wisdom was the visible symbol
of the Christian faith that guided the Emperor's hand. On
the unity of that faith depended the unity of the Empire.
Justinian believed it to be his duty under God to make all men
Christian and to make all Christians hold exactly the same
truths to be eternal. Procopius thus describes his Emperor's
obsession:

'In his concern to bring all men to one belief in Christ he
wantonly destroyed the rest of mankind, and this under the
pretence of piety. For it did not seem to him to constitute murder if those who died happened to be of a faith different from
his own. Tribonian once said to him that he was very much
afraid that one day the Emperor might suddenly be gathered
up to Heaven. He accepted such praise, or rather mockery, as
quite in keeping with his own fixed ideas of himself.'

Justinian followed the example of the first Christian Emperor
by regarding the affairs of Church and State as completely
interdependent and under his single control. The œcumenical
councils of the Church, summoned by Constantine and his successors, had defined the nature of right belief or Orthodoxy,

and their canons had the force of law. Those who offended against them were criminals. The offenders might be un-redeemed pagans, unrepentant Jews, or Christian heretics. The pagans were not organised for survival, but their philosophies were still potentially dangerous. In 529 Justinian ordered the Platonic Academy in Athens to be closed. The pre-Christian classics could still be taught, but only in Christian institutions. Pagans were commanded to receive instruction in the Christian faith and to be baptized, and there was a purge of the aristo-cracy in Constantinople. Christian Orthodoxy was a necessary qualification for entry into the higher civil service, although exceptions were made for some who had rendered themselves indispensable. The lawyer Tribonian held his own private beliefs; while Procopius tells us that John of Cappadocia used sometimes to go to church and mumble blasphemous words throughout the liturgy. Others simply paid lip-service to the state religion as the easiest way out. Procopius claims that the residents of his own city of Caesarea, though unable to see much sense in Christianity, took to calling themselves Chris-tians in order to be on the right side of the law.

The Jews within the Empire, though condemned as an abominable race, were treated rather more tolerantly than the pagans. But the principal sufferers under Justinian's bigotry were the Christian heretics. For they were a more obstinate and clamorous minority, particularly in the eastern provinces of Syria and Egypt, whose loyalty to the Roman Empire had never been whole-hearted. Large numbers of their inhabitants clung to the monophysite theology which had been condemned as un-orthodox at the Council of Chalcedon in 451; and the attempts of Emperors and Patriarchs in Constantinople to bully them into accepting the party line in doctrine killed what little allegiance they felt to the Empire. Some of Justinian's predeces-sors had tried to work out a doctrinal formula that would satisfy all parties and prevent the complete secession of these immensely valuable provinces from the central government. But many of the leaders of the Church, and especially the Popes in Italy, objected to any kind of compromise with heresy and pointedly declared that the Emperors had no right to interfere in theological matters. Justinian had little time for such nice distinctions between theology and politics. To bring the eastern heretics to heel he preferred the direct method of persecution to that of persuasion. But he was embarrassed by the fact that his wife Theodora was herself a monophysite by conviction and not afraid to shelter and protect her husband's victims. In this dilemma Justinian vacillated, now tolerating the heretics, now satisfying the Popes and the more extreme of his bishops by terrorising them.

In 553, five years after Theodora's death, he convened yet another council of the Church, at which the so-called Three Chapters—the works of three long-dead theologians which the monophysites thought to be misguided—were belatedly denounced. It was a concession of sorts. But the Pope and the Western bishops refused to subscribe to the imperial ruling on the matter. The co-operation of the Pope was important; for he represented the cause of Orthodoxy and so of imperial policy in the western provinces which had so recently been rescued from the rule of Arian heretics. But in Justinian's view Popes and Patriarchs alike were ultimately his servants and agents. Pope Vigilius was therefore brought to Constantinople and held prisoner until such time as he saw fit to sign the Emperor's edict concerning the Three Chapters. Such treatment of the bishop of the old capital of the Empire alienated the sympathy of the western provinces from the Emperor. And, as things turned out, Justinian's attempt at compromise was in any case unacceptable to most of the monophysites in the eastern provinces. So far as the peace and unity of the Church was concerned therefore Justinian lost on all counts; and he was brought to realise that it was easier to impose political unity on his subjects than uniformity of belief. But the example that he set of an Emperor who was determined to force his will on the Church was to be secretly or openly admired and emulated by many of his successors.

The separatism of the provinces of Syria and Egypt, manifest-
ing itself in theological deviation, was one of the many serious
problems that Justinian left unsolved when he died in 565. For
his followers the aftermath of Justinian's reign was like the
costing and clearing process after a lavish theatrical production
run at a crippling loss. The boasted liberation of Italy from
the Goths was seen to have reduced the country to penury, and
left the way open for new invaders. Rome was a desolate and
deserted ruin, its walls and buildings shattered, its great aque-
ducts broken. Milan had been completely destroyed and its
inhabitants massacred. In the country-side agriculture had
ceased, and the survivors could hardly meet the taxes to pay
for their own defence. Procopius is eloquently bitter about the
hardships imposed by the Emperor's financial officials, not
least by the iniquitous but highly efficient John of Cappadocia.
Another writer of the time, a retired clerk called John Lydus,
declares that many citizens were less horrified by the prospect
of a foreign invasion of their land than by the news of an
impending visitation from the imperial tax-collectors. It is
fair to say that Justinian took many steps to check and prevent
extortion and corrupt practices among his officials. But the
oppressive system of taxation which he had inherited had to
be maintained without relaxation and often supplemented to
meet the phenomenal expense of his multifarious projects.
There was no possibility of building up reserves; and at the end
of his reign the treasury was exhausted and the economy
ruined. His successors were simply unable to find the money
to support the structure that Justinian had created.

But the cost had been in men as well as in money. The population of the Empire had fallen disastrously in the sixth century.
An epidemic of bubonic plague in 542 had swept over Asia
Minor and the Balkans. 300,000 people are said to have died
in Constantinople alone; and the movement of troops spread
the disease to Africa, Italy and western Europe. But the most
serious effects were felt on the comparatively neglected eastern
and northern boundaries of the Empire. In the east the Persians

had been allowed to reach the Mediterranean coast for the first time since the days of Darius and Xerxes. Justinian contrived a third settlement with them in 562, but only at the expense of paying a humiliating tribute; and the rash refusal of his successor Justin II to pay it led to a new outbreak of war. But at the same time, to the north of Constantinople, the Danube line, the natural frontier of the ancient Roman world, was beginning to break before a new flood of barbarians.

The hard lesson that Justinian's heirs had to learn was that the survival of the Greco-Roman Christian civilisation depended on the security of the eastern and northern approaches to Byzantium and not on the territorial integrity of the old Roman Empire. With the resources left to them they had little option but to cut their losses in the West. Sicily and South Italy for long remained Roman or Byzantine. But Spain was gradually retaken by the Visigoths, and in 568 the Lombards began their invasion of Italy from the north. Ravenna and Rome were soon isolated from each other and in danger of being cut off from Constantinople. Justinian's nephew, Justin II (565–578), and his successor Tiberius II (578–582) made heroic efforts to stem the tide on all fronts. Justin sent an army over to Italy in 575, but it was defeated; and three years later the Lombards laid siege to Ravenna. Tiberius bought them off and encouraged the Franks to attack them from behind. But in the same year 578 the Persians rose to the attack again and invaded Armenia.

The greatest of Justinian's immediate successors was Maurice, who came to the throne in 582 after a victorious campaign against the Persians. Maurice concentrated all his remaining resources on righting the balance of power in the east; and by 591 he had achieved a more stable situation on the Persian frontier than had existed for many years. Like Justinian, he then felt free to turn to the protection of his other provinces. It was mainly due to his efforts that anything at all was saved from the wreck of Justinian's western conquests. Maurice transformed Ravenna in the north of Italy and Carthage in North Africa into the two fortified outposts of Roman rule in the West. Each was placed under the command of an Exarch acting as the Emperor's deputy, and combining the functions of a general with those of an administrator. This was something like government by martial law. The clear distinction between civilian and military organisation in the provinces, upheld since the days of Diocletian and Constantine, was abolished. War was acknowledged to be a chronic condition in the West and not merely a temporary evil; and to meet the necessities of war without drawing on the central reserve of imperial troops the local populations of Italy and Africa were conscripted as soldiers to defend their own terrain. The Exarchates of Ravenna and Carthage provided the pattern for the system of military administration that was to be so successfully extended over the eastern provinces in and after the seventh century. Their creation saved what could be saved in the west. But in the north it was already too late to save the day.

Even before the Lombards began to move down into Italy, new waves of invaders wholly alien to the Roman and the Christian tradition were threatening the very heart of the Empire from the north. Ever since the days of Augustus the inner line of defence in central Europe had been the Danube. Roman interests further afield, and above all the overland trade routes to the East, were protected by outposts and by alliances in the Crimea and in the Caucasus mountains, between the Caspian and the Black Sea. So long as the Danube frontier was held Roman civilisation was safe. For the city of Constantinople was really only vulnerable to attack from the landward side. But in the course of the sixth century developments were taking place far beyond that frontier over which the Emperors had no control. The Avars, an Asiatic people related to the Huns and the Turks, had moved westward from their home in central Asia as refugees from a tribe of Turks more powerful than themselves. They were a savage and warlike people and they carried all before them. By about 550 they had reached the northern shores of the Black Sea and the territory above the lower reaches of the Danube. There they began to lord it over the multiracial hordes who had already settled beyond the Roman pale, the Gepids, the Antae, the Bulgars and Slavs.

The various tribes collectively known as the Slavs had been descending to this district for many generations from their home north of the Carpathian mountains. In the first part of the sixth century ever greater numbers of them arrived, as the Germanic people migrated to the West. The Slavs were an industrious, agricultural race with no great ambitions of military conquest and no yearnings for urban civilisation. But by Justinian's time they had begun to make periodic and highly destructive raids over the Roman frontier into Macedonia and northern Greece. If left to their own devices the Slavs might eventually have been tamed, converted and absorbed into the Roman world. But this was made impossible by the arrival of the Avars on the European scene. For the Avars provided the aggressive drive and the leadership which the Slavs themselves lacked.

Justinian had welcomed the arrival of the Avars, considering them to be useful potential allies. In 558 he signed a treaty with their chief granting them the privileged status of *foederati* of the Roman Empire, as his predecessors had done with the Goths in similar circumstances. It was a maxim of imperial diplomacy that one enemy should be played off against another; and, as a sixth-century historian put it, 'whether the Avars are victorious or whether they are beaten, in either case the Romans stand to gain'. It was thus as allies of the Emperor that the Avars destroyed or subdued all his enemies north of the lower Danube; and before long all the hitherto disunited tribes of Slavs and others were either annihilated, like the Gepids, or forced to acknowledge Avar supremacy.

The Avars and their Slav subjects claimed as the reward for their services the right to settle on Roman soil south of the Danube. So long as Justinian was alive the claim was ignored. But Justin II refused to treat such dangerous allies as equals, and in the end was obliged to buy them off by payment of tribute in 574. Towards the close of the century Avars and

Slavs took to pouring across the Danube in overwhelming numbers into what is now Jugoslavia and Greece. The great fortifications and castles that Justinian had built to defend the northern limits were undermanned or deserted and cut off from Constantinople. The Slavs, experts at cultivating waste land, began to settle permanently in Greece. A later Greek Chronicle records that by the year 587 the whole of the Peloponnese except for Corinth and the east coast had been occupied by Slav colonists. The Emperor Maurice, with the instincts of a soldier, decided that the only solution to the problem was to strike at its roots. In 592, as soon as he had brought the Persians to terms, he led his armies over the Danube into the heart of the Avar territories. For several years he waged ceaseless and often successful war on the new barbarians. But the victories that he won were achieved in isolated battles; nor could he ever recruit enough soldiers to gain the advantage over such apparently limitless numbers. The people of Constantinople resented the cost and strain of a war which seemed to produce so few results. Dissatisfaction mounted and at length the army on the Danube mutinied and proclaimed Phocas, a junior officer, as Emperor in November 602. Phocas marched on the capital, and Maurice lost his throne and his life.

The short reign of Phocas brought disaster nearer than ever before. There was disorder and anarchy on every hand. The Persian king at once went to war to avenge the murder of the Emperor Maurice whom he had regarded as his friend. The Slavs were left free to roam unchallenged through the Balkans. But the Empire seemed paralysed and uncertain of its direction. The comparatively untroubled succession to the throne which had been secured by heredity or by nomination since the very beginning of the sixth century had now been disrupted by revolution. What little sense remained of continuity and stability in the imperial government was shattered; and the usurper Phocas was no better than an illiterate roughneck who put his own interest before all other considerations. Almost his only consistent friend was Pope Gregory the Great, who had fallen out with the Emperor Maurice. The Pope approved of the renewed persecution of the monophysites in the East and of the manner in which Phocas stifled the pretensions of the Patriarch of Constantinople. But the way in which Phocas rose to power was itself symptomatic of a fundamental unrest in society. Justinian's expensive attempt to put the clock back to the old Roman order of things, unpopular enough in his own day, had produced a delayed reaction. It was not only malice that drove Procopius to describe Justinian as a destructive and dangerous meddler. Another contemporary, John of Ephesus, had felt that the end of the world was at hand. The old order was indeed passing away and a new order was coming into being. The usurpation and tyranny of Phocas may be regarded as violent manifestations of the change that was taking place. The process had been temporarily arrested by Justinian's exploits, but it had been hastened by their disastrous consequences. The transition was only completed when men had painfully brought themselves to accept the idea that they were no longer living in a world whose shape and concepts had been determined by Augustus and the founders of the Roman Empire. If the age of Justinian was the last phase of that Roman Empire, the age that followed was the first phase of the new and vigorous social, political and economic structure which it is convenient to call the Byzantine Empire. But the turn of the sixth century was the climax of the transitional process.

The change, which affected almost every aspect of life in the late sixth century, can most vividly be seen by glancing at the map. By 602, when Phocas murdered his way to the throne, the dominions of the Roman Empire which Justinian had laboured to reintegrate were scattered and sparse. The main concentration was in the eastern Mediterranean. But even here it was a question whether the remnants could be saved from inundation by the Persians and the Slavs. For both made use of the Empire's weakness at the start of the seventh century. A deliverer from the Persians was to appear in the person of the Emperor Heraclius. But the Slavs remained as permanent settlers in the Balkans, and their presence was like a wedge driven down the middle of the universal Empire.

The barbarian invasions of the sixth century were similar in character but different in consequence from those which had marked the collapse of the Roman Empire in the West one hundred years earlier. The Goths in Italy and the Franks in Gaul had to some extent recognised and even admired the old Roman order of the world. Their rulers were not above accepting honours and titles from the Emperors in Constantinople. But the new barbarians, the Lombards in Italy, the Avars and Slavs in the Balkans, were and remained outsiders. The Lombards never acknowledged any kind of indebtedness to Constantinople, and were in the end to be subdued not by Romans or Byzantines but by the Franks. Nor were the Slavs ever to be fully absorbed into the imperial structure. The recovery of Greece from the Slavs was indeed achieved by Byzantine armies in the ninth century; but it was a military enterprise directed against a foreign and still pagan race. The division of the Roman Empire into a Greek East and a Latin West had been inherent in its very foundation. Justinian had tried to paper over the crack. But the Lombards in Italy and the Slav occupation of the Balkans in the sixth and seventh centuries made the division. No Emperor could now reunite the two components of the ancient *imperium* or prevent them from drifting apart and developing in their own different ways.

So at the end of the age of Justinian the material world that he had recreated seemed to have crumbled beyond hope of reconstruction. But myths are less easily destroyed than materials; and perhaps the greatest service that Justinian performed for his successors was to infuse new life into the myth that the Roman Empire was a divinely ordained institution destined to admit no limits to its authority and no term to its life. If, after the upheavals of the fifth century, a long run of mediocre Emperors had governed from Constantinople, the ancient Roman concept of a universal *imperium* might have died a natural death. Had there been no Justinian the East Roman or

Byzantine Empire might have declined in the sixth century to the status of a Greek and oriental kingdom, cut off in theory as well as in fact from the West. But after Justinian this was no longer possible. The recovery of the lost western provinces was always on the agenda of his Byzantine successors, even when the project was manifestly absurd. The myth prevailed over reality. Justinian's contemporary, the sailor Cosmas Indicopleustes, had expressed it in these words:

'While Christ was still in the womb the Roman Empire received its authority from God as the agent of the dispensation which Christ introduced, since at that very time began the never-ending line of the successors of Augustus. The Empire of the Romans thus participates in the majesty of the Kingdom of Christ, for it transcends, so far as an earthly realm can, every other power; and it will remain unconquered until the final consummation. For I am persuaded that although, as penalty for our sins, hostile barbarians may from time to time rise up against Roman rule, yet will that Empire remain invincible through the might of its rulers, so long as they advance and do not retard the cause of the Christian faith.'

This was the myth that inspired the confidence of some of Justinian's greatest followers. There might be defeats and emergencies. But in God's good time the whole œcumenical Empire would once again be restored under the rule of the one true Emperor, regent of God on earth and head of the Christian Church.

BIBLIOGRAPHY

I. *Sources available in English translation*

Cosmas Indicopleustes, *The Christian Topography*, trans. J. W. McCrindle. London: Hakluyt Society Publications No. 98, 1897.

Evagrius, *Ecclesiastical History*, trans. E. Walford. London: Bohn's Ecclesiastical Library, 1854.

D

John of Ephesus, *Ecclesiastical History*, trans. R. Payne Smith. Oxford, 1860.

Procopius, *History of the Wars*; *Anecdota (Secret History)*; *On the Buildings*. 7 vols. London & New York: Loeb Classical Library, 1914–1940. *Secret History*, trans. G. H. Williamson. Harmondsworth: Penguin Books, 1966.

II. Modern Works

Barker, J. W., *Justinian and the Later Roman Empire*. Madison and London: University of Wisconsin Press. 1966.
The most recent work on Justinian in English. A thorough treatment of the political, ecclesiastical and military events of the age, set in the context of the Background and the Aftermath, but rather lacking in discussion of the literary, artistic and scientific achievements of the time.

Bury, J. B., *A History of the Later Roman Empire from the Death of Theodosius I to the Death of Justinian (A.D. 395–565)*. 2 vols. London, 1923; paperback reprint, New York: Dover Publications, 1958. Vol. II gives what is still the best, and most literate, account in English of the reign of Justinian.

Bréhier, L., *Le monde byzantin*, I: *Vie et Mort de Byzance*. Paris, 1948. Book I (L'Empire romain universel (395–717)) provides a convenient, though somewhat disjointed, conspectus of the events of the period.

Cambridge Medieval History, vol. II, ed. H. M. Gwatkin and J. P. Whitney. Cambridge, 1913; revised ed., 1926. Vol. II covers events from the accession of Justinian to A.D. 717 and, though old, is still useful (especially Chaps I and II on Justinian, by C. Diehl, and Chap. IX on the Successors of Justinian, by N. H. Baynes).

Diehl, C., *Justinien et la Civilisation byzantine au VIᵉ siècle*. 2 vols. Paris, 1901; reprinted, New York, 1959. The old standard work on the age of Justinian in French. Highly readable and well illustrated.

Diehl, C., *Théodora, Impératrice de Byzance*. 3rd ed. Paris, 1904; reprinted, 1937.

Diehl, C., *Impératrices de Byzance*. Paris, 1959. This selection from the same author's *Figures byzantines* contains his short but charming essay on the Empress Theodora.

Diehl, C. and Marçais, G., *Le monde orientale de 395 à 1081*. (*Histoire du moyen âge,* vol. III, in *Histoire générale,* ed. G. Glotz). Paris, 1936; 2nd ed., Paris, 1944.

Downey, G., *Constantinople in the Age of Justinian* (Centers of Civilization series, 3). Norman, Oklahoma: Oklahoma University Press, 1960. An excellent short introduction to the history and civilisation of VIth-century Constantinople and the Empire.

Goubert, P., *Byzance avant l'Islam,* I: *Byzance et l'Orient sous les successeurs de Justinien. L'empereur Maurice. II,* 1 and 2: *Byzance et l'Occident sous les successeurs de Justinien. Byzance et les Francs. Rome, Byzance et Carthage.* Paris, 1951, 1956, 1965. A detailed and scholarly history of the Empire and its neighbours in the latter part of the VIth century.

Holmes, W. G., *The Age of Justinian and Theodora.* 2 vols. London, 1905-1907; 2nd ed., 1912. A long, if rather superficial, but still readable and useful work.

Jones, A. H. M., *The later Roman Empire, 284-602: A Social, Economic and Administrative Survey.* 4 vols. Oxford; Basil Blackwell, 1964. This is the most up-to-date and authoritative study of the period, indispensable as a work of reference for any extended research.

Jones, A. H. M., *The Decline of the Ancient World.* London: Longmans Green & Co, 1966. A much reduced and diluted version of the same author's *Later Roman Empire,* but very valuable as an introduction to the problems of the age.

Lot, F., *La fin du monde antique et le début du moyen âge.* Paris, 1927. Trans. P. and M. Leon as *The End of the Ancient World and the Beginning of the Middle Ages,* New York and London, 1931 (reprinted as paperback in Harper Torchbooks (No. 1044), New York, 1961. A most stimulating account of the period, though tending to concentrate on the decline of the Empire in the West.

Rubin, B., *Das Zeitalter Justinians,* I, Berlin, 1960. Planned as a four-volume work, only the first volume of this comprehensive study of the age of Justinian has so far appeared.

Stein, E., *Histoire du Bas-Empire,* II: *De la disparition de l'empire d'Occident à la mort de Justinien (476-565).* Revised edition by J.-R. Palanque. Paris, Brussels and Amsterdam, 1949. A basic and indispensable work of scholarship.

Ure, P. N., *Justinian and his Age.* Harmondsworth: Penguin Books, 1951 (Pelican No. A-217). An invaluable and highly readable short introduction to the subject.

Vasiliev, A. A., *Justin the First, An Introduction to the Epoch of Justinian the Great* (Dumbarton Oaks Studies, 1). Cambridge, Mass., 1950. As the only monograph on the reign of Justinian's predecessor, this provides the most authoritative account of the generation before the age of Justinian.

III

Heraclius, the Threats from the East and Iconoclasm: A.D. 610-843

CYRIL MANGO

Most historians today hold the view that for the Eastern Mediterranean region in particular the division between Antiquity and the Middle Ages is to be placed in the seventh century and, more precisely, in the reign of the Emperor Heraclius (610–641). Broadly speaking, the world-order of Late Antiquity was based on the equilibrium of two super-powers: on the one hand, the Roman Empire embracing the entire Mediterranean basin, on the other, the Persian Empire that extended from the river Euphrates to the confines of India. Though traditionally hostile to each other, these two powers were, more often than not, in a state of peaceful confrontation, if not peaceful co-existence, and intercourse between them was kept to a minimum. Outside these two Empires and some minor states clustered round them (the Caucasian principalities, South Arabia, Abyssinia), the rest of the known world this side of India was a fluctuating sea of barbarism.

The erosion of this world-order was naturally a gradual process. Even so, it may be said that when Heraclius mounted the throne over the dead body of the detested Emperor Phocas in 610, the Byzantine Empire was still a recognisable approximation of what the Roman Empire had been in better days. True, Italy was being slowly conquered by the Lombards, and, more important, the entire Balkan peninsula had only recently been overrun by a host of Avars and Slavs. But the Empire still stretched from the Euphrates to Gibraltar, and within its boundaries the old Graeco-Roman way of life continued, trade-ships sailed from one end of the Mediterranean to the other, polite literature was being written, and there were even some small pockets of ancient paganism left.

Heraclius found the Empire bereft of both resources and

soldiers. In this state of unpreparedness he was forced to fight a
desperate war with Persia—a war which, as it turned out, was
to be the last between the two great powers. This conflict has
entered the realm of legend and been presented to us as one
between two religions, between Christianity and Mazdaism. In
vain Heraclius begged for peace: the only reply he obtained
from the Persian King Khusro II was, 'I shall not spare you
until you have renounced the Crucified one, whom you call
God, and bow before the Sun.'[1] And so the Persians overran
Syria and Palestine, Egypt and Asia Minor, and they carried
off from Jerusalem the major relic of Christendom, the True
Cross. At length Heraclius was roused to fight back. For six
years he campaigned on the eastern border carrying the war
into the very heart of Persia, undeterred even by the news that
Constantinople was under siege (626), until he crushed the
enemy at the battle of Nineveh and burnt his Mazdaean fire-
temples. The Persian Empire collapsed; the True Cross was
miraculously rediscovered and returned to Jerusalem; and, just
as God had laboured for six days and rested on the seventh, so
Heraclius, after the six-year war, returned triumphantly to
Constantinople and was acclaimed by the people.[2]

But he ought not to have rested. The year 622, when Heraclius set out on his legendary Persian expedition, was also the year
of the Moslem Hijra, when the Prophet Muhammad fled from
Mecca to Medina, effectively the beginning of the religion of
Islam. Heraclius had scarcely time to put his reconquered
domains in order, when an entirely unexpected enemy, the
Arabs, burst in upon him. In the face of this new danger, the
great emperor showed an uncharacteristic passivity. After a few
blows had been struck, he made up his mind to abandon Palestine and Syria, and brought the True Cross to Constantinople.
With incredible rapidity the Arabs advanced in all directions
and, while they absorbed the prostrate Persian Empire and
reached the mountains of the Caucasus in the East, they simul-
taneously invaded Egypt, took Alexandria, and began their in-
exorable expansion along the coast of North Africa. By the time

Heraclius was dead, a thousand years of history had been undone.

The man who, in his old age, presided over these disasters, the Emperor Heraclius, remains an enigma. His effigy adorned with an immense beard and an equally impressive moustache is familiar to us from his coins. We know that he was capable of the greatest exertions and showed remarkable gallantry in the field; that he incurred much censure for having contracted an incestuous marriage with his niece Martina; that he suffered acutely from hydrophobia and dropsy. His descendants shared a streak of violence and insanity.

With the death of Heraclius in 641, the Byzantine Empire may be said to enter a dark tunnel from which it emerged, greatly changed, some two centuries later. The events of these two centuries are known to us only in the barest outline, for the simple reason that the writing of history came to a halt. By the term 'history' I mean a connected and reasoned narrative after the manner of Thucydides or Polybius. The events of the preceding century had had their historians in the persons of Procopius, Agathias and Theophylactus Simocatta whose narrative ends in 602. The deeds of the Emperor Heraclius were described not in prose, but, appropriately enough, in epic verse by George of Pisidia. And here, if we include George in our list, the succession of historians breaks off and it is not resumed again until the tenth century. What little we know about the intervening dark period has to be pieced together from monkish chronicles, lives of saints, acts of ecclesiastical councils and from outside accounts—Arabic, Syriac, Armenian.

The story that emerges from these sources is mainly one of constant fighting. How desperate the situation was in the East may be gauged from the fact that in 663 the Emperor Constans II seriously considered setting up the capital of the Empire at Syracuse—a plan which, had it been carried out, would have considerably altered the subsequent history of Europe. However, Constans was shortly thereafter assassinated in his bath (668) and his successor remained at Constantinople.

The initial impetus of the Arab advance did not slacken for about a century. Bit by bit, all Byzantine North Africa was lost until, in 711, the Arabs had reached the Atlantic. Twice Arab fleets laid siege to Constantinople—the first time from 674 to 678, a five years' blockade, the second time in 717–718, but both attempts failed. The main theatre of war lay, however, in Asia Minor. Here the mighty range of the Taurus mountains in the South East was the natural bulwark of Byzantine possessions. Again and again Arab armies crossed this range and advanced towards Constantinople, towards the Black Sea, towards the Aegean, but they did not manage to establish a permanent foothold on the plateau of Asia Minor. For more than two centuries major expeditions and seasonal raids went on with monotonous regularity until a large part of the country was reduced to a state of desolation.

While the Arabs were the principal enemy of the Empire, they were not its only enemy. About the year 680 the Turkic Bulgars established themselves in the country that is today Bulgaria, a country that had already been settled by Slavs, and there they set up the only organised and dynamic state to emerge in the Balkans during the early Middle Ages. By the eighth century Bulgaria had already become a serious threat to the Byzantine Empire, the more so as there was no easily defensible frontier between them.

The Heraclian dynasty died out with Justinian II, whose interrupted reign was filled with brutal and apparently arbitrary massacres. Several short-lived emperors then succeeded one another until a strong man emerged in the person of Leo III, a native of northern Syria. It was he who broke up the second Arab siege of Constantinople in 718. This averted the worst of the danger, but the situation remained highly critical since most of Asia Minor was still in the enemy's hands.

Leo III, who was under the influence of a group of eastern bishops, must have thought long and hard about the disasters that were constantly befalling the Empire. Why was it that the Almighty had ceased to defend his own Chosen People? Why had the impious Arabs been so singularly successful? A volcanic eruption in the Aegean Sea in the year 726 appears to have convinced the Emperor that God was indeed mightily angered, and that the sin for which the Christians were being chastised was that of idolatry. He accordingly decided to ban the veneration and use of religious images throughout his dominions. This ban, called Iconoclasm, was officially promulgated in 730 and, except for one fairly long interruption, remained in force until 843.

A great deal of scholarly investigation has been devoted to Byzantine iconoclasm. The question that has been troubling historians is basically this: how can it be that a great empire was rent for more than a century by the trivial issue of whether or not pictures of Christ and the saints should be used for devotional purposes? Was not iconoclasm a façade for something else? Might not the iconoclastic emperors have been enlightened social reformers who chose to attack a particularly glaring manifestation of popular superstition? Or was their object to confiscate the enormous riches of the monasteries and to bring monasticism into disrepute seeing that the monks were the chief defenders and propagators of icon-worship? Or was iconoclasm somehow an expression of the class struggle? To my mind, all such explanations are deeply anachronistic. I believe that iconoclasm was precisely what it appears to be on the surface, namely a religious controversy concerning the use and abuse of Christian portraiture. But there are two considerations that ought to be mentioned.

First, we must remember that the use of icons assumed a disproportionate importance in the Byzantine world from about the second half of the sixth century onwards, and that this was contrary to the teaching of the Early Church. Not only were icons the material focus of popular devotion, the substitutes, as it were, of Christ and the saints, they were also deliberately exploited by the government for their own purposes. When Heraclius sailed to Constantinople to seize power in 610, he ordered icons of the Virgin Mary to be affixed to the masts of his ships. In 626, when Constantinople was being besieged by the combined forces of Avars and Persians, icons were prominently displayed to help in the defence of the city as the following passage from a contemporary homily shows:

'The Patriarch caused sacred images of the Virgin holding in her arms her Son, our Lord, to be painted on all the gates of the city that faced west. They were like the sun of righteousness scattering darkness with its rays, since it was from the west that the progeny of darkness [the Avars] had come. In so doing the Patriarch was, as it were, crying out in spiritual language to the throng of barbarians and to the demons that led them: "It is against these, O alien nations and demonic tribes, that your war is directed. Your pride and insolence will be crushed by the command of a woman, the Mother of God, whose Son sank the Pharaoh and his whole army in the Red Sea and reduced all demons to impotence." '8

And yet, in spite of these supernatural defenders, one Byzantine city after another fell to the godless enemy. The icons had betrayed the trust placed in them. Was not this proof that the Christians, like Israel of old, were guilty of idolatry by offering their worship to pieces of wood and metal, and that they were being punished for this very reason?

The second consideration we ought to bear in mind is that iconoclasm was not limited to the Byzantine world. It was broadly a Near Eastern phenomenon, a wave of puritanism that swept over Jews and Arabs, Syrians and Armenians alike. One may be tempted to describe it as the delayed reaction of the Near East to the pagan Graeco-Roman world. Indeed, we happen to know that the source of Byzantine iconoclasm lay in the Near East, in Palestine and Syria to be precise. This emerges from an official account that was presented to the Seventh Œcumenical Council of the Church in 787:

'When [the Caliph] Omar died [720], he was succeeded by Yezid, a frivolous and unstable man. Now, there was in

Tiberias a certain leader of the lawless Jews, a magician and instrument of soul-destroying demons called Forty-Cubits-High.... Apprised of Yezid's frivolity, this man went up to him and attempted to foretell him the future. Having in this way won the ruler's confidence and familiarity, he said to him: "I wish, O Caliph, to indicate to you a certain way by which you will win an extension of your life and will remain here to rule for thirty years, if you follow my advice." Won over by the promise of longevity, the senseless tyrant replied, "Anything you suggest to me I shall readily do." ... Whereupon the Jewish magician said, "Give orders without delay or postponement that a circular letter should be sent throughout your dominions to the effect that every kind of pictorial representation, be it on boards or in mural mosaic or on holy vessels or on altar-cloths, or anything else of the kind that is found in Christian churches should be suppressed and entirely destroyed; not only these, but also all the effigies that are set up as decoration in public places." It was a devilish plot on his part to have added "every kind of effigy" because he tried in this way to avoid the suspicion of being hostile only to us [Christians]. The wicked tyrant was easily persuaded and sent out emissaries throughout his lands to pull down the holy icons and other images, and in this manner he denuded the churches of God that were in his dominions, and this happened before this plague had reached our country. And since the God-loving Christians were unwilling to destroy holy icons with their own hands, they took to flight, and the task was delegated by the emirs who had been sent out to accursed Jews and miserable Arabs. And so they burnt the holy icons, and some churches they whitewashed, while others they scraped down. When the unworthy bishop of Nacolia and his followers heard of this, they imitated the lawless Jews and the impious Arabs and set about insulting the churches of God.'[4]

While this account may be biased and embroidered, the factual information it contains can be largely substantiated.

And this same Bishop of Nacolia was, incidentally, one of the ecclesiastical advisers of the Emperor Leo III.

The controversy about icons moved immediately on to a theological plane since it was considered to involve the reality of Christ's Incarnation, and it generated a vast body of polemical literature. For a brief explanation of the issues that were at stake we may turn to St. Theodore the Studite (d. 826), one of the subtlest defenders of icon-worship:

'All of us may be depicted, for he who cannot be depicted is not a man but some abortive creature; indeed, every living thing that has seen the light of day is naturally depictable. Hence, Christ, too, may be depicted, even if the godless [i.e. the Iconoclasts] think otherwise and so deny the mystery of the salutary Incarnation. How, indeed, can the Son of God be acknowledged to have been a man like us—He who deigned to be called our brother—if He cannot, like us, be circumscribed?[5] How could He have been born according to the law of nature if He was not similar to His own mother? For if He was not circumscribed, then it was not out of her virginal blood that He fashioned a temple unto Himself, but had a body made in heaven, as was the opinion of the heretic Marcellus[6] and other impious men before him. It also follows that His mother was not really His mother, but one falsely so called; that He was not similar to us, but of a different nature; furthermore, that Adam has not been redeemed. For how can a body of earth be resurrected in a body of a different kind, when it has been proved that like is saved by like? Further, it would follow that death has not been swallowed up [cf. 1 Cor. 15:54] and that worship according to the [old] Law has not been abrogated, including the necessity of circumcision and all the rest.

'Seest thou into what an abyss of impiety the Iconoclasts have been precipitated by believing that Christ should not be depicted on panels? Surely, theirs is a Jewish faith. Hence, they do not acknowledge either the Mother of God or any of the saints, for by refusing their portraits they abominate the per-

sons portrayed. Honour or dishonour done to an image is conveyed to its prototype, as St. Basil says.'[7]

Iconoclasm met with stiff opposition not so much from the
official Church hierarchy as from the monks. These holy men
proved immune to argument and persuasion, and so the calen-
dar of the Orthodox Church became adorned with a new set of
martyrs and confessors. Some were put to death; many were
maimed or exiled; while others were subjected to public ridicule by being forced to parade through the Hippodrome, each
monk holding a woman by the hand. As far as we can judge,
iconoclasm never commanded much popular support throughout the Byzantine Empire except in the army. The first two
iconoclast emperors, Leo III and his son Constantine V, proved
to be highly successful soldiers and so seemed to vindicate the
correctness of their inonoclastic doctrine. We would dearly like
to know more about Constantine V, an indefatigable soldier
and a subtle theologian, who swept the Arabs out of Asia Minor
and nearly succeeded in crushing the growing power of Bulgaria. But his religious opponents suppressed all favourable and
even fair-minded evidence about him and made him almost
into a non-person, if I may use the modern expression. Here
is his portrait, or rather his caricature, as recorded by the
chronicler Theophanes:

'It is fitting that I should describe the lawless actions of his
[Leo's] most impious and miserable son [Constantine], actions
more iniquitous and abhorrent than his father's, and that I
should describe them truthfully as I am doing this in the sight
of God who sees everything.... Now this pestilential, crack-
brained, blood-thirsty and most savage beast achieved power
by usurpation and not by law, and first he parted company with
our God and Saviour, Jesus Christ, His immaculate Mother and
all the saints. Perverted by magic, licentiousness, by bloody
sacrifices and the excrement of horses, yea, by self-abuse and
the invocation of demons, he was reared from his earliest
youth amidst every kind of soul-corrupting pursuit. When he

inherited both his father's empire and his father's wickedness, need I say how much evil this foul man immediately brought forth and fanned its flames until it became a conflagration? The Christians who saw this were seized with great despondency.'[8]

It was this devil in human form, this persecutor of monks who, for thirty-four years, laboured ceaselessly for the security of the Empire. But as security returned, iconoclasm lost support. When, in 780, power passed to the regent Empress Irene, the worship of icons was re-introduced and officially confirmed at the Seventh Œcumenical Council in 787. It took another major calamity, namely the two disastrous defeats inflicted on the Byzantine armies by the Bulgarian Khan Krum in 811 and 813, to bring iconoclasm back. The Emperor Leo V, an Armenian who ascended the throne when the Bulgarians stood before the walls of Constantinople, is represented as holding the following discourse with his friends:

'Why is it that the Christians are suffering defeat at the hands of the gentiles? In my opinion it is because the icons are worshipped and for no other reason; and, therefore, I intend to destroy them. For you can see that all the emperors who have recognised them and worshipped them have died either in banishment or in battle, while those emperors who have not worshipped them, and they alone, died a natural death on the throne, and each one of them was splendidly buried in the imperial sepulchres at the church of the Holy Apostles. I wish, therefore, to imitate the latter and destroy the icons, so that both I and my son should live a long life, and so that my line should remain on the throne until the fourth and fifth generations.'[9]

Leo's personal hopes were not fulfilled since he was murdered in 820 and did not found a dynasty, but iconoclasm remained in power for another generation, until 843, when it was officially abandoned, to the delight of pious believers.

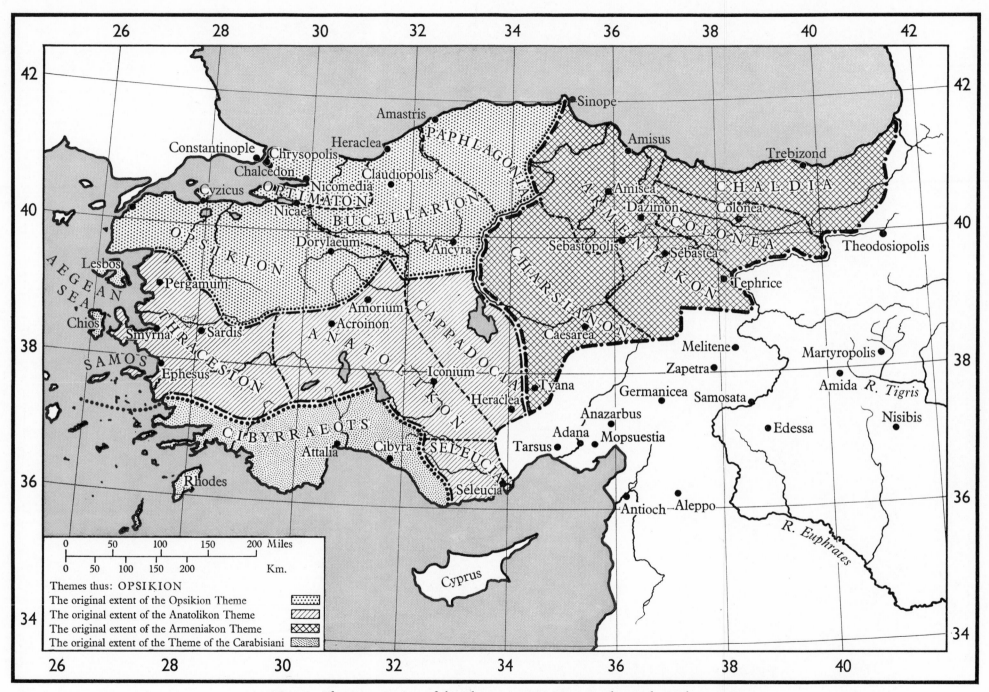

Map 2   The Organization of the Themes in Asia Minor in the VIIth–IXth centuries

Map 2. The Organization of the Themes in Asia Minor in the VIIIth–IXth centuries.

In the early ninth century, and especially in the reign of the last iconoclast Emperor Theophilus, we notice a distinct cultural uplift in the Byzantine Empire. This uplift was nearly contemporary both with the Carolingian Renaissance in the West and with the flowering of Arabic letters under Harun al-Rashid in the East. It would be an exaggeration to say that higher education had been entirely interrupted in the dark days of the eighth century: the story that Leo III burnt the university of Constantinople together with its professors has no foundation in fact. A number of cultivated persons did receive their schooling in the eighth century, such as the Patriarch Tarasius (born about 730), the Patriarch Nicephorus (born about 758), St. Theodore the Studite (born in 759), and Theophanes the chronicler (born in 760). All these men belonged to a small clique of civil servants (a fact to which I shall presently return) and may, therefore, be compared to a man of the same social class, the Patriarch Photius (born about 810) whose formative years were spent in the reigns of Michael II and Theophilus. What emerges from such a comparison is not a change in intellectual orientation, but a considerable extension of culture and a multiplication of books available for study: Photius's famous *Bibliotheca*, composed, it would seem, in 838, contains the summary of 279 works, both Christian and ancient Greek. This phenomenon should certainly be connected with the introduction of the minuscule script—a library script more compact and less time-consuming than the earlier uncial—first represented by the so-called Uspensky Gospels of 835 (Leningrad, Public Library, cod. 219). A campaign was then begun to salvage and recopy the literary remnants of classical antiquity, and it is to this campaign, which continued through the ninth and tenth centuries, that we owe in large measure the preservation of the Greek classics.

As darkness lifts, we can survey the condition of the Empire in the ninth century and compare it with what it had been before the Arab onslaught. The Byzantine world in 843 was a much smaller world than it had been in 610 when

E

Heraclius came to the throne: smaller in geographical extent, sparsely populated and limited in its outlook. True, the Empire still retained certain possessions in the West, namely southern Italy and Sicily as well as the Dalmatian coast, and there was some movement of persons to and fro, mainly ecclesiastics, soldiers and civil servants. The journey from Constantinople to Italy was, however, both dangerous and time-consuming. Greece, whose reconquest by the Empire was begun about the year 800, was still largely in the hands of independent Slavonic tribes, while farther north lay the hostile state of the Bulgars. Overland communication across the Balkan peninsula was consequently disrupted, so that contact with Italy was maintained only by sea—a sea that was infested with Arab pirates. A few lives of ninth-century saints cast an interesting light on the difficulties of east-west travel. Thus about the year 820 St. Gregory the Decapolite tried to make his way from Ephesus to Constantinople and thence to Italy. At Ephesus, which was an important port at the time, he had trouble in finding a ship because the captains were afraid of being attacked by Moorish pirates. He managed nevertheless to reach Proconnesus (in the Sea of Marmora) and then, abandoning his plan of proceeding to Constantinople, he sailed west to Christopolis (Kavala). There he went ashore and immediately fell into the hands of Slavic brigands. Having escaped from them, he made his way to Thessalonica and thence to Corinth where he once again had difficulty in persuading a captain to take him to Sicily because of the fear of Arab pirates. Finally he reached Reggio.[10] Even after the conversion of Bulgaria to Christianity in 864 travel across the Balkan peninsula remained very hazardous. St. Blasius of Amorium, who was also bound for Rome, made the mistake of going overland via Bulgaria where he was sold into slavery. Set free by his master, he made for the Danube where he was captured by brigands, then abandoned in a desert place. He returned to Bulgaria and it was only by attaching himself to the entourage of a bishop that he succeeded in reaching Rome.[11]

While Byzantium was thus cut off from the West, the Papacy, hard pressed by the Lombards, naturally gravitated towards the rising power of the Franks. The coronation of Charlemagne in 800 struck a blow at the most fundamental tenet of medieval political philosophy: the oneness of the Roman Empire. We do not know whether the news caused much of a stir in the government circles of Constantinople: our chief Byzantine informant, Theophanes, devotes only a few lines to Charlemagne's coronation. What appears to have interested him most is that 'Karoulos' was, contrary to Byzantine ritual, anointed from head to toe. He also reports Charlemagne's proposal of marriage to the Empress Irene with a view to 'uniting the East and the West'.[12] Irene appears to have been interested, but the project was frustrated by one of her eunuch advisers, and shortly thereafter she was dethroned.

In reality, the Byzantines were much less interested in Charlemagne and the Papacy than they were in the affairs of their immediate neighbours—the Arabs, the Bulgarians, and the Turkic Khazars established on the north coast of the Black Sea. Contact with the Arabs, while usually hostile, was nevertheless uninterrupted: prisoners were taken and exchanged, embassies travelled to and fro. Byzantine generals who rebelled against their own government were sure of finding friendly support from the Arabs: thus, the usurper Thomas the Slav who seized most of Asia Minor in 820–821 made a pact with the Caliph al-Ma'Mūn and had himself crowned by the patriarch of Antioch, a prelate residing in Arab territory. In the reign of Theophilus there developed a curious cultural rivalry between the courts of Constantinople and Baghdad. The same Caliph al-Ma'mūn tried unsuccessfully to obtain the services of the foremost Byzantine scholar of the time, Leo the Philosopher, while Theophilus built for himself a replica of the palace of Baghdad.

The administrative machinery of the Empire was, of course, profoundly affected by the disasters of the 'dark period'. The separation of civil and military authority, which was a fundamental principle of the Late Roman system, had perforce to be abandoned. This trend was foreshadowed by the creation in the reign of Maurice (582–602) of the exarchates of Ravenna and Carthage where both civil and military power was vested in the hands of the Exarch—a step which transformed those western possessions into semi-independent principalities and fostered in them the growth of local loyalties. Then, starting in the reign of Heraclius, Asia Minor was divided into a number of military areas, called *themes*. Each of these was governed by a commander (*strategos*) who could call on the services of men with hereditary freeholds to form an army at any time. This was in fact equivalent to a permanent state of military alert. The theme-system was gradually applied in the course of the eighth and ninth centuries to all territories under the effective control of the Empire. The institution of this reform was made possible by the massive transplantation into the Empire of various peripheral populations, mainly Armenian and Slav, which henceforth constituted the core of the army.

Whereas the theme-system has received a great deal of scholarly attention, there is a related question of some importance that has not been explored, namely the fate of the pre-existing aristocracy. It is true that in the Early Byzantine period there was no hereditary nobility since nobiliary titles were tied to specific posts and were not inheritable; nevertheless, an aristocracy combining wealth, culture and high office did inevitably develop. If we ask what became of this aristocracy during the seventh and eighth centuries, we shall have to answer that it was probably to a large extent liquidated. Several emperors— Phocas, Justinian II and Leo III—massacred members of the nobility and confiscated their property. Even more decisive at a time when wealth was based on landholding must have been the ravaging of the countryside by the enemy and the large-scale distribution of plots to the thematic soldiers. While the greater part of the old aristocracy must have faded out because of financial ruination, a small kernel nevertheless remained. Thus, the Patriarch Germanus (715–730), who unsuccessfully

opposed the promulgation of the iconoclast doctrine by Leo III,
was descended from the family of Justinian I. It is also recorded
that the Emperor Philippicus (711–713) 'lunched with citizens
of ancient lineage'.[18] It is probably this small remnant of the
old aristocracy that, serving in the civil service and the Church,
assured some continuity in the transmission of polite learning.
Most of the intellectual figures of the eighth and early ninth
centuries (to whom I have referred on page 51) went through
the same career and were often interrelated by marriage.
The Patriarch Tarasius, son of a prefect of Constantinople,
held the post of *protoasecretis* (First Imperial Secretary) before entering the Church; he was, furthermore, the great uncle
of the Patriarch Photius, who was likewise *protoasecretis*.
The Patriarch Nicephorus, son of an Imperial Secretary, held
himself the same post as the subordinate of Tarasius. St Theodore the Studite was the son of a treasury official and was destined for a career in the civil service; his uncle, St. Plato, had
also served in the treasury. St. Theophanes, son of a governor
of the Aegean islands, held in his youth the palatine rank of
spatharios. These were men of some substance who owned
estates in near-by Bithynia (which is perhaps why they had not
been financially wiped out by the Arab invasions), who had
some kinship with the imperial family (St. Theodore the
Studite was the cousin of the Empress Theodote, wife of Constantine VI; Photius was somehow related to the Empress
Theodora, wife of Theophilus) and who were, broadly speaking, Greek.

Quite different in character was the new military aristocracy
that rose to prominence in conjunction with the establishment
of the theme-system. We have only to read the annals of the
two dark centuries to encounter at every step outlandish names
like Mizizios, Saborios (Shapur) the Persian, John Pitzigaudes,
Barisbakourios, Salibas, Bardanes Tourkos. Of the newcomers,
only the Slavs can be described as barbarians; the others—
Armenians, Syrians, Persians—belonged to developed civilisa-
tions that were not Greek. That is not to say that the cultural

level of the new military élite stood very high. Here, for example, is the characterisation of one of its members, Michael II, a native of Amorium in Asia Minor, who became emperor in 820:

'He abominated Hellenic education, and as for our religious one, he held it in such contempt that he would not even allow young men to do their schooling for fear that having thereby acquired alacrity of eye and speech somebody might show up his own ignorance and force him to take second place: for he was so slow in putting letters together and in pronouncing syllables that it took his sluggish mind longer to read his own name than it would another man to read a whole book. . . . On the other hand, he had great regard for the things he was familiar with. He was able to foretell whether new-born pigs would grow up into fat animals or the opposite; he knew how to stand safely close to horses that kicked and how to give a wide berth to recalcitrant donkeys; he was an excellent judge of mules . . . and of the fecundity of sheep and cows. . . . Such were the studies and the attainments not only of his youth, but also of his maturity.'[14]

In judging the culture of ninth-century Byzantium, we must remember that we have before us a situation roughly analogous to that of British India. For just as in India English was the language of the administration and also served as a kind of Esperanto because of the linguistic diversity of the local population, so in Byzantium a species of Greek was the official language and the only possible link between the heterogeneous populations of the Empire. When Leo V spoke to Bardanes Tourkos he must have done so in Armenian; when he spoke to Thomas the Slav, he may have had to rely on camp Greek. These are matters that we can only guess at: all of our information comes from Greek sources whose artificial idiom hides and distorts the reality of the times.

The decline of urban life is another feature of the period under review. If we cast a glance at a map of the Later Roman

Empire, we perceive that the most flourishing and culturally active cities of the *pars Orientalis*, such as Alexandria, Antioch, Beirut, Damascus, Caesarea of Palestine, and Gaza were situated in lands that subsequently fell to the Arabs. Thessalonica was a beleagured outpost in the midst of Slavic territory. Asia Minor was subjected for more than two centuries to such intense devastation that its walled cities must have served mostly as places of refuge. Nicomedia lay in ruins.[15] Ephesus had greatly contracted since its heydey in the Roman period. Amorium and Ancyra, whose importance seems to have been military and administrative rather than economic, were both devastated by the Arabs in 838. In short, only one city worthy of the name was left in the Byzantine Empire—Constantinople. Whatever remained of the central government machinery, of industry, education and learning was concentrated within its walls. This was the City, the Polis with a capital P, the New Jerusalem, the repository of the holiest relics of Christendom, the centre of the world. We can readily understand not only the pride the Byzantines felt for their City, but also their anxiety for its safety: for they knew that on the fate of Constantinople hinged the fate of Christendom. The Patriarch Germanus expressed this thought in connection with the Arab siege of 717–18:

'Such dangers our City had never before experienced, and not our City only, but the whole world that is inhabited by Christians. For it may be acknowledged without any doubt that Christ's entire flock would have been in the same peril as ourselves had the godless Saracens attained the goal of their expedition against us [i.e. the capture of Constantinople].'[16]

Within Constantinople lay the potentialities for a political and cultural revival. Whether this renewal of vigour was due to the efficiency of the new military system or to the infusion of fresh blood into the Empire or simply to the decline of Arab aggressiveness after the caliphate had been moved from Damascus to Baghdad in 750, is the kind of question that historians will not tire of asking even if they are unable to solve it. The fact remains that in 843 Byzantium stood on the threshhold of an era of expansion. The defeat of iconoclasm was widely interpreted as the suppression of the last of the major Christian heresies: Christ could be seen in the flesh once more, true religion had triumphed. And if Christianity had returned to its ancient purity, there was no obstacle to political success. The task of the Byzantine emperors was henceforth to repair the damage of the seventh and eighth centuries, to recreate the universal Christian Empire of Constantine, Theodosius and Justinian. This ideal objective was not abandoned for several centuries to come.

NOTES

1. Theophanes, *Chronographia*, ed. C. de Boor (Leipzig, 1883), p. 301.

2. *Ibid.*, p. 327.

3. L. Sternbach, *Analecta Avarica* (Cracow, 1900), p. 8. The homily is probably by one Theodore Syncellus.

4. Mansi, *Sacrorum Conciliorum ... collectio*, XIII (Florence, 1767), col. 197 ff.

5. The Iconoclasts claimed Christ to be uncircumscribable (*aperigraptos*) and hence unpaintable (*agraptos*).

6. Bishop of Ancyra in the 4th century.

7. Epist. II, 23, Migne, *Patrologia graeca*, XCIX, col. 1188 f.

8. *Chronographia*, p. 413.

9. Scriptor incertus de Leone Bardae filio, Bonn ed. (along with Leo Grammaticus), p. 349.

10. F. Dvornik, *La Vie de Saint Grégoire le Décapolite* (Paris, 1926), p. 53 ff.

11. *Vita S. Blasii Amoriensis, Acta Sanctorum*, Nov. IV. p. 660 ff.

12. *Chronographia*, pp. 473, 475.

13. Theophanes, *Chronographia*, p. 383.

14. Theophanes Continuatus, Bonn ed., pp. 49, 43 f.

15. Ibn Khordâdhbeh in M. J. de Goeje, *Bibliotheca geographorum arabicorum*, VI (Leyden, 18889), p. 77.

16. V. Grumel, 'Homélie de S. Germain sur la délivrance de Constantinople', *Revue des études byzantines*, XVI (1958), p. 193 f.

BIBLIOGRAPHY

For Heraclius' reign in particular it is necessary to go to general histories and N. H. Baynes' article in *The Cambridge Mediaeval History*, vol. 2, G. Ostrogorsky *History of the Byzantine State* chapter II, and A. A. Vasiliev *History of the Byzantine Empire* chapter IV are recommended.

Alexander, P. J., *The Patriarch Nicephorus of Constantinople*. Oxford U.P., 1958.

Bevan, E., *Holy Images*. London, Allen and Unwin, 1940.

Bury, J. B., *A History of the Later Roman Empire from Arcadius to Irene (A.D. 395 to 800)* 2 vols. London, Macmillan, 1889.

Bury, J. B., *A History of the Eastern Roman Empire from the Fall of Irene to the Accession of Basil I (A.D. 802–867)*. London, Macmillan, 1912.

Christensen, A. E., *L'Iran sous les Sassanides*, 2nd ed. Copenhagen, 1944.

Grabar, A., *L'iconoclasme byzantin. Dossier archéologique*. Paris, 1957.

Lombard, A., *Constantin V, empereur des Romains (740–775)*. Paris, 1902.

Martin, E. J., *A History of the Iconoclastic Controversy*. London S.P.C.K., 1930.

Pargoire, J., *L'église byzantine de 527 à 847*. Paris, 1905.

Pernice, A., *L'imperatore Eraclio*. Florence, 1905.

Runciman, S., *A History of the First Bulgarian Empire*. London, Bell, 1930.

Vasiliev, A., *Byzance et les Arabes*. I. *La dynastie d'Amorium (820–867)*. Brussels, 1935.

IV

The Age of Conquest, A.D. 842-1050
ROMILLY JENKINS

In this section I shall consider Byzantine history from the middle of the ninth century to the middle of the eleventh. I have called this period 'The Age of Conquest', since it saw the second and last serious attempt on the part of the Byzantine Emperors in Constantinople to achieve political control by military means over the territories, both in the west and in the east, that had once been governed from Rome by Augustus and Trajan.[1] This was an attempt to put into practice what had always been true in theory; namely, that the new rulers in Constantinople were the rightful inheritors of all the old Roman Imperial dominion. They in fact derived their own authority from the Emperor Constantine the Great, who had in A.D. 330 moved his capital to the ancient city of Byzantium, newly rebuilt as Constantinople.

According to Byzantine imperial theory, this universal Roman sovereignty over Europe and Asia was preordained by Almighty God, who had granted to the Empire, in His good time a dominion without end in space or duration.[2] When therefore the new Romans of Byzantium drove the Saracens out of Tarsus and Antioch by 969, and then reduced the free and independent state of Bulgaria to Byzantine provinces by 1019, they were not, in their view, committing aggression. On the contrary they were merely taking back what was, in the sight and by the decree of God, their own.

It is most important to note this. Political considerations of a purely temporal character would instantly have exposed the essential foolishness of spending twenty years, and submitting the Empire's resources to a ruinous strain, in order to conquer a vast territory which could, in the long run, not be held, short of a miracle. But it was in miracles that the Byzantines believed. Their policy was dictated by their wonder-working Lord. If Byzantium had been content to fortify her eastern frontier as it had been at the close of the conquests of John Courcouas (944), or even at the death of Nicephorus Phocas (969); if she had been content to leave Bulgaria as a free and friendly state, merely erecting an impregnable barrier to invasion from the north; if she had then been content to develop her foreign trade, backed by an imperial navy such as was maintained by Basil I, and to exploit her internal resources; who can say whether there might not still be a Greek-speaking state on the Bosphorus? This could not be. Faith and fact clashed once more, and faith as usual won the day. *To epithumetikon* was confounded with *to ephikton*, what was desirable with what was possible. For to God, all things are possible. And here I should like to quote some brilliant comments of Paul Lemerle[3] on the results of the Age of Conquest, which reinforce what I have been saying. 'Triumph everywhere; but at what a price: and discreetly encircled by black borders which could only expand! Crete had to be besieged eight months before the Saracens would release their prey; and it needed twenty years for Basil II to reduce Bulgaria. Bulgaria was at last annexed; but at once other invaders from the north crossed over the Danube. Armenia was annexed, but at once the Seljuqid Turks took possession of Ani. In the west, Byzantium could profit by the void—so to say—which lay between Carolingians and Ottonians, but the Normans were the chief beneficiaries. In the east, she could profit by the decline of the Abbasid caliphate; but the Turks profited most by this. In the middle-eleventh century, so brilliant in so many respects, when it seemed that for Byzantium time stood still, was she after all mistress of her own destiny?'

This second attempt to restore the old Roman Empire was, in the long run, no more successful than the earlier one which had been made by Justinian I in the sixth century. In the year 1025 the Byzantine Empire was great, strong and rich. In less than fifty years, in 1071, its might was irreparably broken on the field of Manzikert.⁴ But this does not detract from the splendour, the valour and the statesmanship of the two centuries from 842 to 1025, which are our subject in this section. They were the most glorious era in Byzantine history.

To grasp the immediate objectives of the Age of Conquest it is helpful to look at the position of Byzantium on a map. In the mid-ninth century Byzantium controlled Asia Minor, behind a fluctuating frontier which stretched from a little east of Trebizond to a little west of Tarsus. In Europe, Byzantium controlled Thrace and the southern part of the Balkan Peninsula, that is, modern Greece;⁵ as well as some maritime cities in Dalmatia; Venice; South Italy; and the island of Sicily. Crete was in Saracen occupation, and Cyprus was a demilitarised island under joint Byzantine and Saracen control.⁶

That was the position in 842; in less than two hundred years, by 1025, the eastern frontier of Byzantium ran east to Armenia and Lake Van, and far to the south of Antioch and Aleppo. Crete and Cyprus were once more Byzantine provinces. Italy south of the Papal State was firmly held. Above all, the Balkan frontier no longer ran from Thessalonica westwards to the Adriatic, but from the Black Sea along the Danube and the Save rivers, and enclosed all the once proud and aggressive empire of the Bulgars. The only setback to this expansion had been the loss of Sicily to the Saracens in 902; and even Sicily was partially re-conquered in 1040.

The secondary objectives were also in a fair way to being attained. Byzantine political influence was paramount in Armenia and Georgia, and scarcely less potent in the Russian state of Kiev and in the Muslim caliphate of Egypt. Moreover, when the Emperor Basil II died in Constantinople in 1025, Rome herself and Italy seemed to be his for the taking, and he was preparing an expedition to take them. In all these areas the Byzantine cultural impact was no less obvious than the political. Nor had these triumphs been won—as had the earlier ones of Justinian—at the cost of depopulation and economic ruin. On the contrary: the rural economy of Asia Minor and Greece was exceedingly prosperous, and the Byzantine treasury was over-flowing.

What were the tools which lay to the hands of the great Byzantine conquerors of the tenth century? They were two. First a people of diverse stocks who, after three centuries, had been welded together into a unified whole, partially, at least, Greek-speaking, and inspired by the doctrine of Christian imperialism. Second, out of this population, a splendid army of *native* origin, drilled and trained in provincial army corps by able and courageous officers, who, by long tradition and intermarriage, had become a military caste that dominated all Asia Minor. This army was stiffened by a small but well-equipped and highly paid force of imperial guards, recruited from the hardiest nations surrounding the imperial borders. Amongst these the axe-bearing Northmen of Scandinavia and Russia were, from the tenth century onwards, pre-eminent.[7] But the shock troops of the Age of Conquest were the native Byzantine heavy cavalry, the so-called 'cataphracts'. Both horse and man were cased in steel or hide, a system of armament learnt by the Romans from the east. The offensive arms were lance, sword or mace, and bow. The trooper lived on his freehold agricul-tural property, cultivated by his kinsmen;[8] and out of its revenue he or his parents supplied his own horse and armour. He himself was continually drilled in a squadron of his own friends and countrymen, and knew his own native officers familiarly. Such was the formidable army which routed the gallant but undisciplined hordes of Saracens and Bulgars; and even worsted the Normans from the north and the west, first in Bulgaria and then in Italy.

It is important to note that nearly all the provincial nobility, and a large proportion of their finest troops, were of pure Armenian stock.[9] The noble clans intermarried with one an-other, as aristocracies tend to do. After the depopulation of Asia Minor by Justinian's wars, the Heraclian and Isaurian emperors of the seventh and eighth centuries had recruited

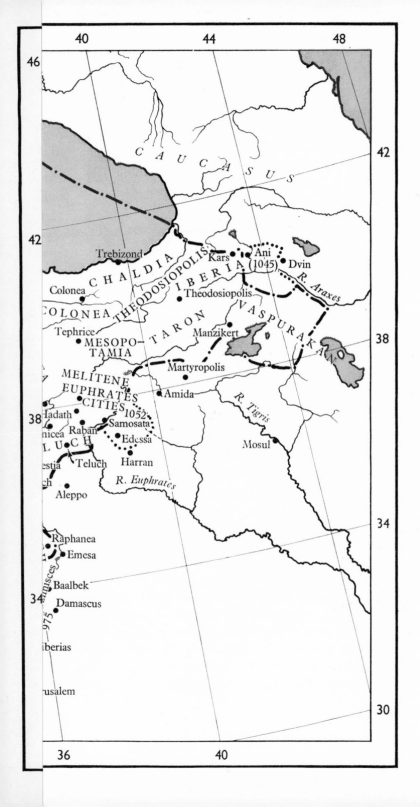

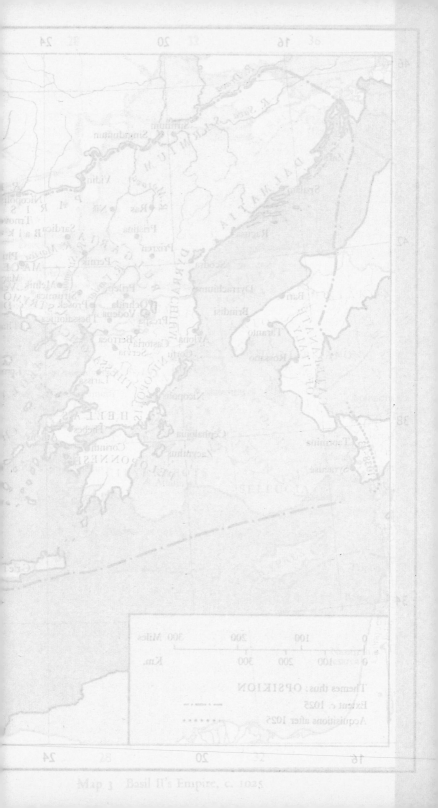

Map 3 Basil II's Empire, c. 1025

Armenian and Slavonic settlers into this area by hundreds of thousands. The Byzantine empire owed its rejuvenation to these new stocks, but to each in a different way. To say that the Slavs restored the agriculture, while the Armenians fought the enemies of Byzantium is a broad generalisation, to which many exceptions can be made; but in essence it is true. In any event, the upper strata of each immigrant stock quickly learnt to speak the language of the empire, that is, mediaeval Greek: though byzantinisation made slower progress among the Slav and Armenian peasantry. The peasant-emperor Basil I, for example, spoke Armenian as his first language:[10] and Slavonic was still spoken in parts of southern Greece as late as the fourteenth and fifteenth centuries.

The sovereigns who presided over the Age of Conquest were known as the 'Macedonian Dynasty'. It was founded in 867 over the bodies of two murdered rivals, by Basil 'the Macedonian', that Basil I whom we have just mentioned; and it was so called because Basil had been born in Macedonia, or, more properly, in Thrace. His father was certainly Armenian and his mother was very probably Slav;[11] and it was wholly appropriate that in him should be united the two chief strains which made for Byzantine greatness. His house ruled for one hundred and eighty-nine years, until the death of his great-great-granddaughter Theodora in 1055; and it acquired in this long period a unique prestige. In later centuries the direct descendants of the Macedonian dynasty came to include the Russian princes of Kiev, a German Emperor, Otto III, and the Bourbon kings of France. When, in the middle of the eleventh century, Basil's line became extinct, the Byzantine historian and statesman Michael Psellus summed up the achievement of the Macedonian dynasty in some memorable words:[12] 'I doubt if any family has ever been so much beloved by God as theirs has been: and this is surprising, when you come to think that it was not lawfully established and planted, but rather in slaughter and blood. But, so planted, it took root and flourished, and put forth so many shoots, each laden with imperial fruit, that

F

no other can be compared with it, either in beauty or magnificence.'

One of the remarkable aspects of the history of the Macedonian dynasty was the deliberate and systematic attempts of
its military aristocracy, in the teeth of equally systematic civilian
opposition, to foster and favour the native peasant militia as an
élite amongst the rural population. The success of the Age of
Conquest depended on the success of this policy. The military
aristocrats were not always loyal servants of the Crown, which
many of them coveted and, in the tenth century, two of them
actually usurped.[13] But, so long as the Crown was able to
control or conciliate them, it had at its disposal for foreign conquest a force which, in point of training and morale, was
superior to that of any army of the time.

The following passage was written at the order of the aristocratic usurper Nicephorus Phocas[14] (who reigned from 963 to
969), by one of his aides-de-camp. It certainly dates from his
time, and expresses his opinions and those of his class. This
passage appears as a Standing Order, addressed by the Emperor
to the provincial Military Governors.

'Sir, you are to take order that your soldiers shall receive their
pay without any lapsing into arrears: yes, and other grants,
besides and beyond what law and custom prescribe. So that,
free of all economic embarrassment, they can buy themselves
the very best horses and the rest of their equipment on the same
scale: and thus, with perfect morale and an eager and happy
courage, they will risk their lives for our Holy Emperors and
for all our Christian community. Most urgent and important
of all things making for their courage, is that their households,
and those of the soldiers serving under them, and their retinues,
shall be absolutely exempt from taxation: which privilege was
granted and reserved to them of old and from the beginning, as
you shall find it laid down by the holy and blessed Emperors of
bygone days, and inscribed in their military manuals. Moreover, in addition to such exemption, the soldiers must have

their due of respect, and not be looked down upon or despised. For I am ashamed to tell you that these men are flogged. These heroes, who give their lives in service to our holy Emperors and for the liberty and defence of Christians, are, I repeat, flogged by a rascally crew of tax-gathering riff-raff, who contribute nothing to the common good, but simply oppress and grind the poor, and out of injustice and the blood of many poor men, pile up for themselves gold by the hundredweight. Sir, your soldiers *must not* be at the mercy of the civil jurisdiction in the provinces, to be arrested and scourged like slaves, to be loaded (oh, the misery of it!) with fetters and collars of iron, they who are the champions and, under God, the saviours of Christendom. The law itself expressly states that each officer is to be master of his soldiers, and himself to be their judge. And who else but the Military Governor is master of the provincial soldiery? If the army of our holy Emperors recovers its ancient prestige, and if the cruelties that reduce it to destitution be removed from it, then will it renew its morale and zeal and peace of mind. It will fight with enhanced courage and resolution, and be unconquerable by its enemies. And thus, not only will our holy Emperors defend their own territories, but will also subjugate any amount of enemy territory besides.'

This outburst, one of the most illuminating passages for the social history of tenth-century Byzantium, clearly illustrates the determination of the military nobles to make their soldiers into a privileged caste. To their success in this policy, during some hundred and fifty years, the Age of Conquest was very largely due. No empire such as the Byzantine had been since the age of Heraclius, could hope to expand, or even to survive, on any other principles. But the policy created a socially explosive situation. The civil bureaucracy, who sent out the said 'tax-gathering riff-raff', detested everything military. They saw no reason why the peasant-soldier should not pay his taxes like everyone else. They closed their ranks; and when the last great conqueror, Basil II, died after seeming to have won a stable

peace, they seized power, cut military appropriations to the
bone, and thus brought about the ruin of the empire in the
incredibly short space of fifty years.[15]

The outburst quoted above leads us onto some closer consideration of the remarkable document from which I have
extracted it, the so-called 'Skirmishing Warfare of our Lord
Nicephorus the Emperor',[16] which, I have said, is certainly of
his time and reflects the political and military conditions of the
Empire around the middle of the tenth century. It is almost
wholly devoted to a study of the defence in depth of the eastern
frontier against the annual Saracen invasions; and no one who
wishes to understand Byzantine warfare in the tenth century
can neglect to study it closely. Many—especially the later—parts
of the treatise derive directly from the *Taktika*[17] compiled, it
would seem in A.D. 903, by the Emperor Leo VI, and a suitable
acknowledgement is made for this indebtedness. But the difference between the two works leaps to the eye. The one is the
work of an industrious civilian, the other the work of a serving
officer. The author of 'Skirmishing Warfare' knows his job at
first hand. He enters in detail into such questions as the posting,
provisioning and relief of forward troops, with all the emphasis
on training and discipline and meticulous attention to detail
that we should expect from the best type of army officer. Above
all, in the same tradition, is the insistence that the officer is
there to lead and to care for the soldiers under his command.[18]
The brigadier is to *lead* his men in the field. The general must,
in the hour of defeat, never be first to seek refuge, but must
wait until he sees his men are safe. This kind of doctrine lies
at the bottom of the phenomenal success of Nicephorus I and
John I. And it is in strong contrast to the cowardly conduct of
the general staff at more than one *sauve qui peut* which
occurred during the war against Symeon of Bulgaria (914–
925), when, as defeat was certain, high-ranking officers, whose
resolution might well have turned defeat into victory, turned
their backs and left their men to be slaughtered at leisure.
Viewed in this light, we can better understand the passage

quoted above (which is incidental to the main purpose of the book). It illustrates the tradition among the military families of the Anatolian aristocracy of care for the fighting soldier. And when, in Crete, in 961, the aristocrat Nicephorus Phocas, then commander-in-chief and later usurping emperor, urged his officers to fight for their Christ and their Faith, they answered: 'We will obey your counsel and your orders. With you we will die.'[19] At the rout of the Achelo, for example, on August 20, 917, the commander-in-chief, Leo Phocas, escaped to Mesembria,[20] when he ought to have died (should this have been necesssary) at the head of his men. He committed the very crime interdicted by the most positive of directives by Nicephorus I (de Vel. Bell. 231, 1–5). Physical courage is something that appeals to and inspires everyone. The lesson was learnt.

Exactly the same rules for military discipline as those laid down by Nicephorus are advocated a century later by Cecaumenus, an exemplary commander with a life-time of military experience.[21] Though he wrote when the empire was in full decline, the old traditions were still very much alive. No one, he says, ever became a good officer by indiscriminate flogging any more than by indiscriminate favouritism. What the common soldier wants is justice. Promotion must be by merit. When a soldier has shown gallantry in the field, and has been passed over for promotion, morale is undermined. These maxims may be truisms; but the emphasis laid on them by Cecaumenus shows that they were by his time in danger of being disregarded.

The following passage from Cecaumenus[22] shows how well these veteran officers knew their business:

'Insist above all on your troopers having good horses, arms that are complete and properly cleaned, and saddle-girths and boots that fit. You may be sure that if a trooper has a good horse, a smart uniform and good weapons, he will, if he's brave, become doubly so, and if timid, will still take courage and play his part. But if he's turned out slovenly, with too big a saddle, boots that don't fit him, and a horse that is good for nothing, you may equally take it for granted that, however brave he may be, he will be thinking of nothing but of how to secure his own safety, by running away as soon as he can.'

Two more brief passages from this sterling officer[23] may illustrate the value put by the military on their own dignity; and also their insistence on the superiority of the *native* Byzantine soldiery to any kind of mercenary troops, however brave or highly paid.

'Don't indulge in civilian habits. You can't be at once an army officer and a buffoon. If some officers do act in these ways it is an anomaly, disgraceful to their class. He who talks or jests foolishly is written down and despised for a fool. If a civilian acts like an idiot, nobody knows or cares; but if you, a military officer, disgrace yourself, even in the most trivial fashion, then everyone learns of it at once. I will give you an example. Basil Pediaditis was commander-in-chief in Sicily, and, during some days when work was slack, he took to playing backgammon. Well, this reached the ears of the Emperor [Constantine IX], who wrote to him thus: "Our Imperial Majesty begs to congratulate you on your victories—at backgammon!" You see, his great services were forgotten, and only the minor defect was remembered.'

And lastly, some sage advice[24] in a memorial addressed to the Emperor Alexius I by the same officer.

'Do not promote foreigners to high dignities or commands, unless they are of royal stock in their own countries. If you do, you are certain to devalue both yourself and your Byzantine officers. If you make some foreign nobody into a brigadier or a general, what ranks are left for the Byzantines? You will merely make them hate you. Besides, when the foreigner's countrymen hear of his promotion by us, they will all laugh and say: "We thought this fellow of no account when he was here; but, you see, he has gone to the Empire and got this commission! It is clear that the empire has no good soldiers, and so our man is promoted". In the old days the emperors [he is thinking of Basil II] never ennobled a Frank or a Norseman, or gave him the rank of a count or a marshal. Only very rarely did they make him as much as a major. All the rest served for bread and a coat.'

By such precepts, and such examples, the noble commanders, the adored and revered 'fathers' of their men, trained and cherished their unconquerable cavalry. The most revolutionary reform in cavalry tactics was—in all probability—introduced by the military genius of the Emperor Nicephorus Phocas, though its description should perhaps be ascribed to the most gifted of Basil II's marshals, Nicephorus Ouranos. It occurs as a section 'On the Cataphracts' in a document entitled 'Nicephori Praecepta Militaria'.[25]

In this reform the central battering-ram of the heavy cavalry was drawn up, not in squadron formation, but in a wedge. The front line of this wedge consisted of twenty heavy-armed cavalrymen in line, the next of twenty-four, and so on, until the rear rank would number as many as sixty-four abreast. The whole formation would, ideally, be five hundred in all; but if your general did not command this number of such expensive and expert cataphracts, he could make do with three hundred and eighty-four. However it was to be arranged, each rank proceeding towards the rear was always to be wider by four men than the row in front of it. The whole machine proceeded towards its objective, the centre of the enemy's line at an even trot. It was led by a senior officer out in front, the position doubtless occupied by the Emperor John in the final charge at Silistria in July 971.

One of the most interesting features of the so-called 'triangular regiment' was its use of archery. 'You are to understand',[26] says our author, 'that there should be archers in among the cataphracts, so that these archers can be protected by them.

Ranks one to four of the cataphracts shall not include archers. But from rank five down to the rear they shall: and if the number of your cataphracts regiment be five hundred, they should have one hundred and fifty archers; and if it be three hundred, they shall have eighty archers.'

As for the cataphract himself, he has these three basic articles of dress: a padded or quilted shirt; a cuirass, with shoulder-pieces; and an outside military cloak; or, as it has also sleeves and a hood, we had better call it a 'duffel'. He has a stout iron head-piece; and, as his face is swathed in cloth, nothing of it can be seen but his eyes. The chief weapons of offence carried in the first four ranks are iron maces, with jagged heads, and swords. In the fifth rank and backwards, the men carry lances. The horses must be (and small wonder!) 'stout': since, in addition to carrying the weight of the rider, they themselves are to be encased in an armour of felt and leather, covering both head and body down to the knees, 'so that nothing of the horse's body is seen except his eyes, his nostrils, and his legs from the knee downwards'.

The archers, who are in a square protected by cataphracts, can be less heavily equipped, in corselet and helmet only. Yet even for them it is recommended that their horses shall be cataphract.

It is easy to see that such a force, trained to a marvel, devoted to its leaders, and fortified by prayer ('Lord Jesus Christ, Our God, have mercy upon us! Accept us Christians, making us worthy to rise up for our Faith and our brothers, and to strive unto death! Fortify and strengthen our souls and hearts and all our bodies, O God mighty in battles and incomprehensible in strength, through the intercession of the Mother of God Who bore Thee and of all the Saints! Amen'),—it is easy, I say, to see how such a force would not be easy to withstand. On the other hand, it is easy to see why its efficiency could only be maintained by an emperor who thoroughly understood and believed in warfare. It cost far too much, for one thing. The training of a *corps d'élite* and its equipment with the most

expensive instruments of war, are always expensive luxuries.
Nicephorus II determined that the citizens should pay.[27] Basil II
determined that the rich aristocrats should pay.[28] But the
moment Basil's hand left the tiller, a series of idle and luxurious
sovereigns succeeded, who thought there were better things to
spend money on than cataphracts.[29] Perhaps there were. But
they went far too far to the other extreme: with the result that
the Empire, fifty years later was left defenceless at the very time
she most stood in need of defence.

The other main problem which confronted this system was
the problem of manpower. Even in its hey-day, Anatolia was
underpopulated. The causes were many: and among the chief
of these was the enormous number of monks and nuns, condemned *ex hypothesi* to a life of sterility. Their rights were
jealously guarded. And even at the mortal crisis of the war with
Symeon of Bulgaria, when every man who could bear arms was
needed, and when some monks were conscripted for this purpose, the Church set up a dismal wail of protest. The conquests
of Courcouas between 923 and 944 undoubtedly did something
to restock eastern Anatolia with imported Muslims: and the
Emperor Basil II recruited captive Bulgars into the ranks of his
army in large numbers. These men were not foreign mercenaries. They were Roman subjects, whose recruitment helped to
fill up the depleted ranks of the Roman army. But, even at the
height of this policy, there was—it is to be supposed—no super-
flux of trained or trainable manpower.

Now, what use did the conquerors make of their 'New
Model'? The topmost point of courage and military expertise
was reached in the brilliant campaign of the Emperor John I
in 971 against the Northmen of Russia, who had invaded Bulgaria and were a direct threat to Constantinople itself. John
threw them back to Silistria, on the Danube, brought them to
bay there and defeated them in six separate engagements.[30]
The next passage from the contemporary historian, Leo the
Deacon, describes the first of these.[31] Note the emphasis laid
on the Byzantine cavalry *as cavalry*, a force which they

regarded as superior to any infantrymen, however gallant. The Russians fought only on foot, as the Saxons fought at Hastings.

'In the earlier clashes, neither side prevailed. The Russians felt it to be unendurable that they, who held among their neighbours a record of unbroken victory, should now lose it shamefully to the Byzantines, and they fought with desperate courage. But the Byzantines, for their part, thought it a foul disgrace if, hitherto successful against all opposition, they should now be worsted in a struggle against a foot-soldiering nation who couldn't even ride. The Russians, with their native savagery and spirit, leapt roaring on the Byzantines like men possessed. But the Byzantines fought back with military skill and technical knowledge. Losses on both sides were heavy. By the late afternoon, the issue was still in doubt. The evening star was already sinking when the Emperor John launched his final cavalry-charge on the Russians with devastating effect: "You are *Romans*!" he cried; "Now show your valour in your deeds!" Thus heartened, the cavalry burst out with irresistible ardour. The bugles sounded the charge. The Byzantine battle-cry rang out. The Russians wavered and fled. Their losses were enormous.'

The sixth and last battle of Silistria, which took place in July 971,[32] and in which the Scandinavian Russians or Northmen were finally demolished, marks the summit of Byzantine military skill in the Age of Conquest. Twelve separate charges of the heavy cavalry were indecisive: they were held, and horses and men were hewn down by the indomitable axe-men of the North. At last, a wind began to blow from the south, and raised a cloud of dust before the Russians' faces. The Emperor John saw that his moment had come. He led the thirteenth cavalry-charge in person. And, through the murk, the doomed Northmen heard the drumming of innumerable hooves, and saw the figure of the Emperor John I in golden armour, the Master of the World himself, emerge and bear down upon them. They broke and fled.

It now remains to summarise the stages by which this superb

military machine was used by the Emperors to achieve their objectives: Byzantium's immediate enemies, ever since the VIIth century, were two: the Saracen caliphate on the eastern frontier and the Bulgarian kingdom on the northern. The last of the so-called 'Amorian' emperors, the ill-starred Michael III who reigned from 842 to 867, decisively checked the first of these menaces, by annihilating a strong Saracen force at Poson, near the Halys river, on September 3rd, 863;[33] and he went some way towards neutralising the second, by forcing Bulgaria into the fold of Orthodox (that is, Byzantine) Christianity in 864.[34] Half a century later, after a desperate struggle of eleven years (A.D. 914–925) with the greatest of Bulgarian war-lords, the Tsar Symeon, Byzantium went over to the offensive. During the twenty-one years between 923 and 944, the great Byzantine marshal John 'Courcouas', as the Byzantines called the Armenian Gourgen, broke the iron ring which the Saracens had forged along the eastern frontier. He re-established Byzantine influence in Armenia, captured Melitene and Erzerum, and drove to the south-east far beyond Tarsus; while Bulgaria, under her peaceful Tsar Peter, was reduced to a Byzantine protectorate.

The third great, and almost uninterrupted, course of Byzantine expansion dates from 961 to 1025. During the ninth and tenth centuries, as I pointed out earlier, the training and perfection of the provincial armies was largely the work of the aristocratic officer class in Asia Minor. It was natural that this class should usurp the Imperial Crown, as it did during the years 963–976. The first of these usurpers was the head of the great clan of Phocas, Nicephorus by name. Even before his usurpation he had retrieved the island of Crete from a Saracen occupation which had lasted a hundred and thirty-five years. In six years of rule, from 963 to 969, Nicephorus exposed the weakness of the Saracen caliphate of Baghdad, and won from the Saracens themselves the fearful title of 'The White Death'. He reduced Tarsus, Aleppo and Antioch, and re-occupied the island of Cyprus. His murderer, kinsman and successor, John I, another warrior-usurper, followed his path in the east, after completing his brilliant campaign against the Russians on the Danube, which I have already described. John's campaign, or rather progress, eastwards in 975 put Damascus in Byzantine hands, and brought him in sight of Jerusalem, a Saracen possession since 634. He would have entered the Holy City, with little or no resistance, in 976, had he not died suddenly in January of that year. John I was a military genius of the first order, and his death was a disaster for the Empire. But it made way for the most extraordinary man ever to sit on the Byzantine throne, Basil II.[35] He reigned from 976 to 1025, and he was the legitimate heir, and great-grandson of the founder of the Macedonian Dynasty.

Basil's first task was to take over the aristocratic war-machine, suppress its dangerously powerful commanders, and set it to work for the legitimate, Macedonian, dynasty. It took him about thirteen years to achieve this, in face of repeated revolt and disaster. When he came to power at the age of twenty, he was without military experience or skill. But by 989, he was undisputed master of his army, and can justly be described as the best tactician and organiser in Europe. His achievement was unique. What sort of a man was this, who could first bring under his command the hitherto uncontrollable military aristocracy, and then go on to conquer the Bulgars, Armenians, Georgians, the Saracens from Egypt, and the Normans. Here is a character-sketch by his contemporary, Michael Psellus, who could just remember him as an old man.[36]

'In stature, Basil was something below the middle height, but his body was perfectly proportioned and his carriage erect. When he was on foot he cut a figure not strikingly superior to others; but on horseback he was altogether incomparable. He was of a piece with his saddle, like some equestrian statue from the hand of a most accurate master. When he gave rein and spur to his charger, he sat bolt upright and unbending; or when he drew rein and checked its career, his body leapt up with it as though on wings, and maintained the same vertical posture as the horse reared or plunged. In his maturity, his beard was scanty; but his whiskers were abundant, and the hair grew rough and bushy on his cheeks so as to make a complete circle round his face. It was his habit to twirl it in his fingers when he was moved, or in conference, or buried in thought. This was a characteristic gesture: as was flexing his elbows and clasping his thighs with his fingers. He did not speak fluently, in sculptured eloquence or rounded periods, but brusquely and laconically, more like a peasant than an educated man. His laughter was a guffaw, and it shook and convulsed his whole frame.'

Such was the Emperor Basil II, the great commander who brought the Age of Byzantine Conquest to its close by the total subjugation of Bulgaria,[37] by restoring the northern frontier of the Empire as it had been in the days of Justinian, and by advancing his eastern borders well beyond Lake Van. He died, unmarried on December 15th, 1025. There seemed then to be no limit to the probable expansion of Byzantium. Her armies were invincible, her treasury overflowing. Had Basil lived another ten years, Italy would have been his, and, after Italy, Africa. Yet, in less than fifty years after 1025, Byzantium's power was irretrievably broken. Its armies were dispersed; its territories under the Turkish or Norman power; its treasury bankrupt. Endless explanations have been put forward for this sudden and total collapse. One, already mentioned, was certainly the jealousy of the civil bureaucracy for the military, on whose strength the Empire depended. When this bureaucracy seized power, the equipment and morale of the Byzantine soldiery were neglected, and unreliable foreign mercenaries were employed in their place. Other causes of course contributed. But, whatever these may have been, Basil II at his death had raised the Byzantine Empire to a pinnacle of achievement recalling the greatest days of Ancient Rome.

NOTES

1. Many times emphasised. Put very well, most recently, by Endre von Ivánka, *Rhomäerreich u. Gottesvolk* (Freiburg-München, 1968), pp. 25–49.

2. Vergil, *Aenid*, I, 279. St. Luke's Gospel, I, 33.

3. P. Lemerle, Collège de France, *Leçon inaugurale* (Paris, 1968), p. 15.

4. G. Ostrogorsky, *History of the Byzantine State* (Oxford, Blackwell, 1968), pp. 344–5.

5. For the reconquest of Greece by the Byzantines, see Theophanes, ed. de Boor, I, pp. 456–7, 486.

6. See R. J. H. Jenkins, *Studies Presented to D. M. Robinson* (1953), pp. 1006 ff.

7. V. G. Vasiljevskij, *Trudy*, I, pp. 176 ff.; A. A. Vasiliev, *Seminarium Kondakovianum*, 9 (1937), pp. 39 ff.

8. Ostrogorsky, *History*, pp. 95–98.

9. P. Charanis, *Byzantinoslavica*, 22 (1961), pp. 196 ff.

10. *Vita Euthymii*, ed. de Boor (Berlin, 1888), p. 2.

11. N. Adontz, *Byzantion*, 8 (1933), pp. 475 ff.; 9 (1934), pp. 223 ff.

12. M. Psellos, *Chronographie*, ed. Renauld, I, p. 117.

13. Nicephorus II (963–969) and John I (969–976).

14. *De Velitatione Bellica Nicephori Phocas* (*ap.* Leonem Diaconum, Bonn, 1828), pp. 239–241.

15. Ostrogorsky, *History*, pp. 320 ff.

16. See note 14, above.

17. J. P. Migne, *Patrologia Graeca*, vol. CVII; R. Vári (ed.), *Taktika*, 2 vols, 1917–22, Budapest.

18. *De Vel. Bell.*, p. 231.

19. *Theophanes Continuatus* (Bonn), p. 478.

20. *Ibid.*, p. 389.

21. Cecaumeni *Strategikon*, ed. Vasiljevsky-Jernstedt (St. Petersburg, 1896).

22. *Ibid.*, p. 21.

23. *Ibid.*, p. 20.

24. *Ibid.*, p. 95.

25. *Nicephori Praecepta Militaria*, ed. Julianus Kulakovskij (St. Petersburg, 1908), pp. 10–12. My attention was drawn to this capital work by Mr. James Howard-Johnston, to whom I am also indebted for several illuminating comments on it.

26. *Ibid.*, p. 11.

27. Cedrenus (Bonn), pp. 373–4.

28. Psellos, *Chronographie*, ed. Renauld I (Paris, 1926), p. 19.

29. Ostrogorsky, *History*, p. 320 ff.

30. Leo Diaconus (Bonn), pp. 128 ff.

31. *Ibid.*, pp. 140–1.

32. *Ibid.*, pp. 153–6.

33. Ostrogorsky, *History*, p. 227.

34. *Ibid.*, p. 230.

35. *Ibid.*, pp. 298 ff.

36. Psellos, *Chronographie* I, ed. Renauld, pp. 22–3.

37. Ostrogorsky, *History*, pp. 309 ff.

BIBLIOGRAPHY

See generally, Vasiliev, A. A., *Byzance et les Arabes*. Bruxelles, 1936–1950; Schlumberger, G., *L'épopée byzantine à la fin du 10ᵐᵉ siècle*. Paris, 1896–1905; and Jenkins, R., *Byzantium: The Imperial Centuries*. London, Weidenfeld and Nicolson, 1966.

Bréhier, E., *Vie et Mort de Byzance*. Paris, 1948 (pp. 179–270).

Cambridge Mediaeval History, vol. IV, Part I, Cambridge U.P., 1966. (pp. 105–192 and Bibliography pp. 849–858).

Diehl, Ch., *Byzantium: Greatness and Decline*. Rutgers U.P., 1957 (pp. 40–126).

Ostrogorsky, G., *History of the Byzantine State*. Oxford, Basil Blackwell, 2nd edition 1968 (pp. 210–315).

Runciman, S., *The Emperor Romanus Lecapenus and his Reign*. Cambridge U.P., 1929.

Vasiliev, A. A., *History of the Byzantine Empire*. Madison, Wisconsin U.P., 1952 (pp. 320–350).

V

The First Encounter with the West, A.D. 1050-1204

ANTHONY BRYER

G

Full-length portraits of almost all Byzantine rulers of the eleventh and twelfth centuries survive—the last Macedonians, the Comneni and Angeli. They are shown in ceremonial robes and bearing the symbols of kingship; the setting is invariably the same. If anything their titles and epithets grow more grandiose: 'In Christ God, faithful Emperor and Autocrat of the Romans'. Byzantium's will to survive has often been attributed to such forms, its unbending pretensions and cultural conservatism. But its ability to survive lay elsewhere. In the eleventh and twelfth centuries the Empire was put to its most severe test since the Arab wars and brought to the brink of extinction, but emerged once more as guardian of Orthodoxy and of an antique tradition. The response of these apparently rigid Emperors to changing circumstances was grudging but fundamental, for during these two centuries Byzantine social and political institutions underwent a painful and profound transformation. Behind the continuity of outward forms of government lay a clumsy ability to adapt the Empire to the changing realities of Mediterranean and Eastern politics. So in some ways the Empire, which Western Crusaders regarded as a tiresome and anachronistic survival from the ancient world, was the most youthful state in Europe.

The stages of military disaster are clear enough. Until the 1040s Byzantium seemed paramount. It stretched from Italy to the Euphrates; its resources and machinery of government were unrivalled. But, after the defeat at Manzikert in 1071, the Empire lost the eastern highlands and central plateau of Asia Minor to the Seljuq Turks; the Normans took its last stronghold in southern Italy in the same year. For a century thereafter the Comnenus dynasty held the shrunken boundaries successfully, even brilliantly, but were never able to restore the vast losses. From the 1170s the Turks and Normans resumed their advances and the Balkans rose. In 1204 Constantinople itself fell to an errant Western Crusade, the devastating conclusion to Byzantium's first encounter with the West. The Empire could never be the same again; its eventual destruction was ensured by the events of these two centuries.

But the eleventh and twelfth centuries also contain the seeds of Byzantium's final flowering, and are the most fertile in the long history of its civilisation. Our sources are comparatively abundant and the period has attracted notable historians, but the mystery remains—why, for the first time, did Byzantium fail to contain its new enemies and how is it that these years are associated with one of the most confident of all Byzantine artistic and intellectual revivals? It seemed that the battered old Empire had never been so alive; it thrived on adversity. Such contradictions tell us much about the real nature of Byzantium and its people.

What went wrong? Contemporaries were not at first aware that anything had gone wrong, and in a way they may be right. But certainly there was a failure of leadership between the death of Basil II in 1025 and the accession of Alexius I Comnenus in 1081. This is clear from the pages of Michael Psellus, the attractive chronicler of the eleventh century. Psellus was a sort of universal pundit who bustled round the court for a good thirty years, taking care to nurture his imperial connections. His memories of Basil II were of a plain-spoken and fearfully efficient old soldier. He much preferred the new breed of gentleman emperors who succeeded Basil. Among these Psellus' favourite was Michael VII, his own pupil, whom the court blithely chose to lead the Empire out of the great defeat at Manzikert in 1071:

'Nothing pleased [Michael] more than reading books on all kinds of learned subjects, studying literary essays, pithy sayings, proverbs; he delighted in elegant compositions, subtle combinations of words, changes of style, coining of new words, poetic diction: but above all else, he cultivated a love of philosophy, of books that enrich the spiritual life. . . . Often he surpassed his present historian, whom in preference to all others, he chose as his tutor, and whose name he mentioned with extraordinary honour. Although he does not apply himself to iambics, he dashes them off extempore, and if the rhythm is generally defective, at least the sentiments are sound. In brief, Michael is a prodigy of our generation, and a most beloved character.'

Michael, like many Emperors between 1025 and 1081, was the candidate of the 'Philosophers', Psellus' political and ecclesiastical cronies in Constantinople. They were the guardians of a great bureaucratic tradition which called for a formal and legalistic style of Greek which they were trained to manipulate. This administrative class proved remarkably resilient and, to some extent, was to survive even after 1453 as servants of both Sultans and Patriarchs. For a few decades in the mid-eleventh century the effective instruments of power were in the hands of the 'philosophers', but soon moved to those of their bugbears, the 'colonels' and provincial landowners. This emergent military aristocracy viewed Michael VII rather differently from Psellus:

'The Emperor busied himself continuously with the useless and unending study of eloquence and with the composition of iambics and anapaests; moreover he was not proficient in this art, but being beguiled by 'the consul of the philosophers', [i.e. Psellus] he destroyed the whole world, so to speak.'

This rivalry for power is one feature of the disintegration of the old political system of the Empire, nor does one have to read far between the lines of Psellus' *Chronographia* to find that the thirteen transitory successors of Basil II—like his slightly absurd nieces with whom the Macedonian dynasty petered out, or such dithering academics as Michael VII—were hardly the best leaders against the Seljuqs. European reports of these Turks are disturbing enough: a Spanish Jewish traveller announced that 'They worship the wind and live in the wilderness.... They have no noses'. The Armenians found them terrifying in battle; they galloped down on the Christians, with long hair streaming behind them, reported Matthew of Edessa.

But Byzantium lay only on the fringe of the Seljuq world in the eleventh century; Baghdad and control of the fragile Abbasid caliphate was their real target, achieved in 1055. Thereafter the Seljuqs took Syria and set about dominating the Islamic East. Byzantium had only itself to blame when, instead, a branch of the Seljuqs made Anatolia their centre. For, unlike the Slavs and Arabs in the past, the Seljuqs (and Normans) came at first to raid rather than to settle. For many years the Byzantines seem to have entertained the hope that they could incorporate their new and not very numerous neighbours into the imperial system. But they utterly failed either to resist or to absorb them. Clearly there must be deeper reasons than those which Psellus suggests for the internal collapse of Byzantium in the face of external threats which were less formidable than those to which the Empire had successfully responded in the past.

To look further than the pages of Psellus; it has long been argued that the stability of Byzantine provincial society and the vigour of its provincial defence system lay in the communities of 'independent' peasants who dealt directly with the state. Basil II was the last Emperor who was willing or able to protect these communities from grasping landowners; Romanus III (1028–34) weakened them still further by abolishing the communal tax obligations on uncultivated land, called the *allelengyon*. The argument goes on to state that the political upheavals of the eleventh century and the accession in 1081 of Alexius I Comnenus, candidate of the military party, finally mark the triumph of the great landowners over the old machinery of government and over the old social structure.

From the 1050s tracts of state land, and some of the functions of the state, were surrendered to the care (or *prónoia*, as
they called it) of a landowner for his lifetime. By the early
twelfth century some grants were made in return for military and other services. By the next century some became
hereditary fiefs, not unlike those which the Norman invaders
held themselves. Soon, of course, *prónoia*-holders became re-
luctant to carry out their obligations to the state, the Empire
had to hire more mercenaries with a depleted revenue and the
peasantry steadily lost what independence it had once enjoyed.
These links between land and those who worked it, military
and other services and the diminished institutions of the state,
are known in the West as feudalism. Basically speaking, Byzantium underwent the Western experience in reverse. While the
rulers of France or of England were creating centralised mon-
archies out of a dispersal of authority among their feudatories,
Byzantine rulers, who had once commanded the most centralised state medieval Europe had known, were losing control to
the growing power of their aristocracy. True, the Byzantine
version of feudalism was never to be so thorough-going as the
classic examples of the West. By those standards it was hap-
hazard and incomplete; the obligations of both lords and serfs
were much more confined than those of their Western counter-
parts. But the process certainly undermined the old imperial
system and the long Byzantine tradition of a salaried career
civil service. Alexius I Comnenus made strenuous efforts to restore the administration, but the damage had been done in the
eleventh century by the demands of the military landowners
and the ineptitude of the higher civil servants, like Psellus,
themselves. Increasingly in the next century the administration retreated to the confines of the imperial household and
the provinces were governed at second hand.

But this explanation for the social and political disintegration
of Byzantium in its years of crisis now appears to be more complex than was at first thought. The dating of the stages of
'feudalisation' and the precise degree to which it went are ever

widening questions. It is becoming increasingly difficult to generalise about the Empire, especially after 1025; the provinces were so diverse, the state less monumental than it seems. For instance, the national minorities of the eastern borders had long had what amounted to a feudal system, while in other areas the old 'independent' communities, together with the *allelengyon* levies, survived in some cases into the fifteenth century. Scholars have wondered how 'independent' these communities had been in the first place, for their peasants were always tied to their lands. The protestations of the tenth-century Emperors and of Basil II that they wish to protect 'the poor' against 'the powerful' may simply disguise a competition between the state and the great landowners for manpower. To the hapless peasant the distinction between paying levies to an imperial agent or to a private landowner was perhaps rather academic. And the Hundred Years' War with the Slavs, culminating in the campaigns of Basil II, had certainly over-reached the resources of the state; in terms of manpower Byzantium never really recovered from the cost of his victories. There are indications of a slow, but absolute, decline of population from the eleventh century; peasants rather than land were at a premium.

Other scholars have questioned the connection between the famous 'independent' communities and the imperial defence system, pointing to the embarrassing inefficiency of the provincial levies on almost every occasion they were actually called to service. In some ways the provincial regiments may have been more of a garrison police than a home guard and the high expense of the new cavalry undermined the old system of personal obligations of service. The 'philosophers' cut back expenditure on the army and the old local defence system and provincial military administration collapsed entirely. From the eleventh century the army, and from the twelfth century the Byzantine navy, was to a great extent composed of mercenaries, many hired from the Empire's Norman, Turkish and Italian enemies. They were paid in increasingly debased coin

and in the 1070s, after Manzikert, the *solidus* was more dras-
tically devalued. But in fact the Byzantine economy remained
remarkably stable, or slow to react to outside events, during
the period. The disaster of the eleventh and twelfth centuries
did not take serious effect until the next century, when
the *solidus* also lost its leading position as an East Mediterranean currency. There were fluctuations, but, although indications are scarce, there are enough to show that prices and
salaries in the twelfth century remained much the same as
they had in the tenth, and in a few cases what they had been as
early as the sixth century. The state suffered from a decline of
its available resources, rather than from diminishing money
values.

In general, however, the growth of the Byzantine version of
feudalism stands as a fuller explanation for the Empire's social
and political disintegration than Psellus' view of a simple opposition by the landowning military aristocracy to the bureaucracy of the capital—some of whom, including the first known
prónoia-holder, were themselves great landowners. These
twenty Anatolian dynasties who challenged the 'philosophers'
of the capital were newcomers, but dominated the Empire increasingly from the eleventh century. By the fourteenth century
their survivors, such as the Palaeologi or Cantacuzeni, had
established family networks of positions of authority all over
the Byzantine world. With their immense ramifications they
amounted to ruling clans rather than simple families. Save
that of the Emperor himself, Byzantium had no hereditary
offices. Nevertheless, during the eleventh and twelfth centuries,
it began to have a number of hereditary rulers. Some family
names were to develop almost into the equivalent of titles. The
ties of kinship and the inheritance of the functions of the state
in lands held in *prónoia* became the keys to power.

This process was in some respects paralleled among Byzantium's neighbours. In the eleventh century the Abbasid Caliphs
granted *iqta* holdings to their Seljuq mercenary leaders—in
these land grants and tax farms there are certain resemblances

to the contemporary Byzantine *prónoia*. Some Seljuq and many Turkoman groups settled in Anatolia in clans, each acknowledging a semi-legendary common ancestor and owing allegiance to chiefs through extended ties of kinship. Eventually one great Greek dynasty, the Palaeologan, was to be replaced in Constantinople by a Turkish equivalent, the Ottoman. By 1453 both families had developed almost to the status of a ruling class.

Armenia probably played a crucial role in this process, the origins of which coincide with its conquest first by Byzantium and then by the Seljuqs in the eleventh century. Armenian society had long been fragmented and highly feudalised. The independence of Armenia lay in its disunity; it could only be conquered slowly and piecemeal. Armenian ruling dynasties claimed descent from such ancestors as Sennacherib and David and Bathsheba. The chronicles of their petty courts read like animated genealogies; this is the stuff of Armenian history. Very many of the twenty great Anatolian families which emerge in eleventh-century Byzantium, had Armenian origins; a number of Byzantine fiefs in Central Anatolia were given to Armenian dynasties from the eastern borders. To some extent they must have influenced the Byzantine shift of power from a state bureaucracy to a group of semi-feudal warlords. The degree of Armenian influence upon their Seljuq conquerors has yet to be defined. It is clear enough in some fields such as architecture and decoration and the Armenian theme officials and *prónoia*-holders who became Seljuq *uç beys* (frontier barons) no doubt contributed to political institutions as well. The Danişmends were not too proud to claim Armenian ancestry and thereby inherit the extensive genealogies which were the source of a right to rule in the steep valleys and upland pastures of Eastern Anatolia.

But to detect the beginnings of a fundamental change in political ties and of governmental system in both the Byzantine and Turkish East is not to explain why Byzantium lost Central and Eastern Anatolia, its supposed heartland, so swiftly and

irrevocably in the years after 1071. What *really* went wrong?
The clue seems to lie in what actually happened in those ten
years of Seljuq breakthrough after Manzikert. The imperial
defence system all but collapsed, but the Turks were in no
position to resist determined local opposition. Compared with
other Seljuq conquests of the time, the Anatolian campaign
was an unauthorised sideshow. Yet the Turks overran the
country quite casually, reaching the Aegean for a while. In the
ten years between Manzikert in 1071 and the accession of
Alexius Comnenus in 1081, the pretensions of Byzantium as a
Universal Empire were laid bare and its true nature revealed at
last.

The cultural background to these years is important. It was
one of lively renewal, of great monastic foundations decorated
with expensive mosaics whose style is still confident and monumental. The followers of such uncompromising ascetics as
St. Symeon the New explored the spiritual life anew in the
hermitages of Athos and Bithynian Olympus. Michael Psellus
was now Professor of Philosophy at the refounded University
of Constantinople; he boasted that he had exhausted the learning of the Ancients and was even putting the Fathers of the
Church to rights. And theologians, such as John Mauropus,
were also reviving the teaching of classical philosophers, for
Byzantine humanism and Orthodoxy remained two facets of
the same tradition, linked quite literally, by a common language.

This was essentially a Greek and an Orthodox revival, even
aggressively so, and here perhaps lies a hint of what went
wrong in 1071-81, for the Greeks and the Orthodox were far
from being the only members of the Empire. Basil II's conquests of only fifty years before looked fine on the map, but
in Armenia and in the Balkans they simply turned useful
buffer states and allies into resentful vassals. The Balkan Slavs,
whom Basil had subdued so ruthlessly, had already known
independence and tasted statehood. The church into which
they had been baptised as a means of introducing them to the

Byzantine imperial system had become instead a symbol of their national consciousness. It was only a question of time before they rose against their clumsy conquerors. There were a number of local rebellions, but Byzantium managed to hold the Balkans until the late twelfth century—at a price; the lands through which the Third Crusade passed in 1189 were desolate. In the East, Basil's work was much more short-lived. The Byzantine annexation of the last Armenian kingdom, Ani, in 1045 and the cities of the Euphrates in 1052 coincided with the first serious Seljuq raids over those very borders. Probably the Byzantines had been lured by the commercial possibilities of Armenia, which stood astride a number of important routes, but their expansionist policy there proved disastrous. Bagratids and Artzrunis lost their petty thrones; Armenian refugees moved west to Cilicia and Cappadocia, or started the long trek to Sebasteia, Trebizond, and the Crimean Little Armenia, finding their way up the Danube and into Hungary some centuries later. To those who stayed in the Armenian highlands (almost certainly the majority), both Greeks and Turks were almost equally oppressive. Too often the Empire meant extortionate officials, mercenaries who came to garrison rather than defend the country and hectoring Greek bishops who attacked the Armenian Church, their last national institution. Matthew of Edessa put the Armenian view forcefully:

'Armenia was surrendered to the blood-drinking Turks by the impotent, effeminate, ignoble race of Greeks. The Greeks deposed our true rulers, scattered our defences and sent eunuchs to protect us. Like cowardly shepherds they thought only of themselves when the wolf came. So the Turks broke through and in one year reached the gates of Constantinople.'

An exaggeration, of course, but the Greeks in turn felt just as strongly about the Armenians. One of their ballads ran:

'The most terrible race of the Armenians is deceitful and evil to extremes, mad and capricious and slanderous and full of deceit, being greatly so by nature. On being honoured they become more evil; on acquiring wealth they became more evil altogether. But when they become extremely wealthy *and* honoured, they appear to all as evil doubly compounded.'

In this atmosphere of mutual distaste it is hardly surprising that Basil II's expanded Eastern frontier in Armenia fell swiftly. When the Seljuqs came, some Armenian leaders accepted them with relief; a few even regained their old authority under the new Muslim régime. Others took advantage of the confusion to set up semi-independent lordships which lasted into the twelfth century. There is no doubt that Basil II's victories in Armenia are a direct cause of his successor's defeat there in 1071. Manzikert lies in Vaspurakan, north of Lake Van. In 1022 Basil had removed Sennacherib Artzruni, Armenian king of Vaspurakan, from his island capital of Aghthamar, settling Bulgarian prisoners of war in the province. In spring 1071, on his way to Manzikert, the Byzantine Emperor Romanus IV Diogenes executed the last exiled Artzruni princes on the grounds that they had been 'plotting'. At Manzikert Frankish, Armenian and Turkish mercenaries and private armies of the Greek military aristocracy had every reason to abandon Romanus to his fate. His fate is instructive. Alp Arslan, the Seljuq leader, required only a guarantee of peace and an alliance and sent Romanus back to his capital to obtain it. Instead the new Emperor Michael VII, egged on by Psellus, savagely blinded the defeated Emperor, who died soon afterwards. By doing so, the 'philosophers', not content with largely disbanding the army, virtually forced the Seljuqs to enter Byzantium proper to obtain their terms.

When, ten years later, the dust settled, the Seljuqs emerged holding the central plateau and eastern highlands, while the Byzantines retained the coastlands of Anatolia. Apart from a number of centres in the Ionian West, which Byzantium regained at the turn of the century in the wake of the First Crusade, all the skill of the Comnene Emperors and the doubtful assistance of the Second and Third Crusades could do little to alter the boundary. The campaigns of Alexius (1081–1118), John II (1118–1143) and Manuel Comnenus (1143–1180) only skirted the borders. Even in the 1090s, when the Seljuqs were in disorder, there were no serious attempts to claim the lost lands. For the borders revealed after 1071 are ancient and distinctive. They follow ethnic, geographic and economic lines. Apart from a Greek pocket in Cappadocia, which survived until modern times, the Seljuqs, by showing who was prepared to fight for the Empire and who was glad to escape its intolerable burden and alien culture, brought to light historic national limits which had been disguised by the common rule of the Roman and Byzantine Empires for a thousand years. The Ionian lands and coastal trading stations, colonised during the first millennium B.C., remained Greek—precisely the areas from which the Greek Empires of Nicaea and Trebizond were to arise after 1204. But if the coastlands were largely Greek and the Eastern highlands largely Armenian and Georgian, what was the population of Central Anatolia, where the Seljuqs founded their state? Clearly it was very mixed, including Greek and Armenian elements, to say nothing of Slavs who had been deported there. But basically it was composed of the descendants of the indigenous peoples of Asia Minor, who had been Hellenised in the past and who were now to contribute to the ancestry of the modern Turks. The Seljuqs did not persecute Christians as a policy, yet Orthodoxy all but perished here, while the Armenians clung to their national Church. For the peoples of Central Anatolia the Greek Church had been identified with the State which had demanded so much; many were glad to be rid of it.

But anyone who has had to change buses in Manzikert today and who has followed the routes of Seljuq infiltration, may be forgiven for wondering if the Byzantines were not fortunate in losing that forbidding land. Even in 1071 Central Anatolia was already desolate and thinly populated; there are in fact very few Byzantine monuments there which can be dated after the eighth century. It had not always been so, nor were the Seljuqs responsible for the waste. The destruction of urban life and the replacement of market towns by garrison fortresses can probably be ascribed to the Arab wars of the eighth and ninth centuries, which, year after year, had deeply penetrated the area. The Seljuqs were not really nomadic in the eleventh century; in Persia they had been settled agriculturalists for generations and Seljuq chroniclers boast of the revival of agriculture on the plateau and of the watered gardens of Konya, created out of a desert. But the Greek coastal valleys, which encircled the plateau, were in fact better watered and more fertile; later the Greeks were to export agricultural products for Turkish gold. The valleys were also better wooded and the twelfth-century boundary roughly follows the Anatolian tree-line, above which the finest upland grazing lands in the country run in a great crescent from the Pontic Alps in the north-east to the Taurus in the south-east. The Seljuqs were not primarily pastoralists, but the Turkomans who insulated the Seljuq state of Konya from the Byzantines were nomadic. The Turkomans fought both Greeks and Seljuqs for the grazing, gradually settling in the valley below the pastures. For example one Turkoman group, the Çepni, began working along the northern pastures of Paphlagonia in the late twelfth century, only reaching the modern Russian border six hundred miles to the east in recent years. The settlement which followed 1071 was slow and protracted.

Eventually the events of 1071–81 were to create a largely Greek state out of what had been a multilingual Empire. But this development was delayed for a century by the genius of the Comnene dynasty, the last to make the Byzantine claim to universal dominion more than a mere form.

Alexius I remains the hero of this deceptive interlude, although John II and Manuel were in some ways more remarkable, for his daughter Anna made him the subject of the finest of all medieval biographies. Like all Byzantines, she carried her learning a little ponderously; she was often querulous and on her dignity and she idolised her father. But her book is unforgettable. When the Emperor died in 1118, Anna summoned up all the conventions of Byzantine historical writing, stating the ideals of Comnene scholarship in the first words of *The Alexiad*:

'Time in its irresistible and ceaseless flow carries along on its flood all created things, and drowns them in the depths of obscurity, no matter if they be quite unworthy of mention, or most noteworthy and important, and thus, as the tragedian says, "he brings from the darkness all things to the birth, and all things born envelops in the night".

'But the tale of history forms a very strong bulwark against the stream of time, and to some extent checks its irresistible flow, and, of all things done in it, as many as history has taken over, it secures and binds together, and does not allow them to slip away into the abyss of oblivion.

'Now, I recognised this fact. I, Anna, the daughter of two royal personages, Alexius and Irene, born and bred in the purple. I was not ignorant of letters, for I carried my study of Greek to the highest pitch, and was also not unpractised in rhetoric; I perused the works of Aristotle and the dialogues of Plato carefully, and enriched my mind in the four schools of learning.'

In the pages of *The Alexiad*, the Emperor is described as the epitome of Byzantine kingship. He feared God and was a father to his people. He had little use for the absurdities of Western chivalry and, as an efficient and successful general, preferred to win his victories by patient diplomacy or by simply fooling his enemy. He trained a central professional army and reorganised the civil administration. He travelled ceaselessly, one year over the Via Egnatia to face the Normans of Sicily in the mountains of Albania, the next year to establish the Seljuq boundary in the East. Movingly, Anna reveals the immense physical toll of carrying the cares of a great medieval state almost single-handed for nearly forty years. Alexius faced each

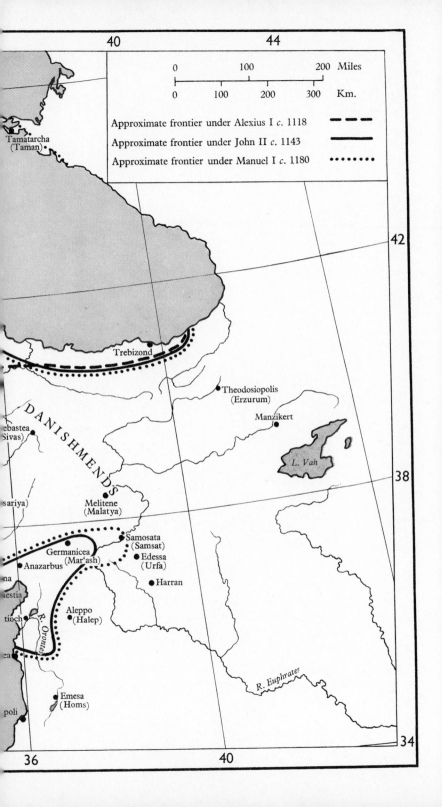

40

44

	0	100	200	Miles

	0	100	200	300	Km.

Approximate frontier under Alexius I *c.* 1118 — — —

Approximate frontier under John II *c.* 1143 ———

Approximate frontier under Manuel I *c.* 1180 ••••••••

Tamatarcha
(Taman)

42

Trebizond

Theodosiopolis
(Erzurum)

Manzikert

D A N I S H M E N D S

ebastea
(Sivas)

L. Van

38

sariya)

Melitene
(Malatya)

Samosata
(Samsat)

Germanicea
(Mar'ash)

Edessa
(Urfa)

Anazarbus

na
Harran

estia

tioch

Aleppo
(Halep)

R. Orontes

R. *Euphrates*

ea

Emesa
(Homs)

poli

40

36

40

34

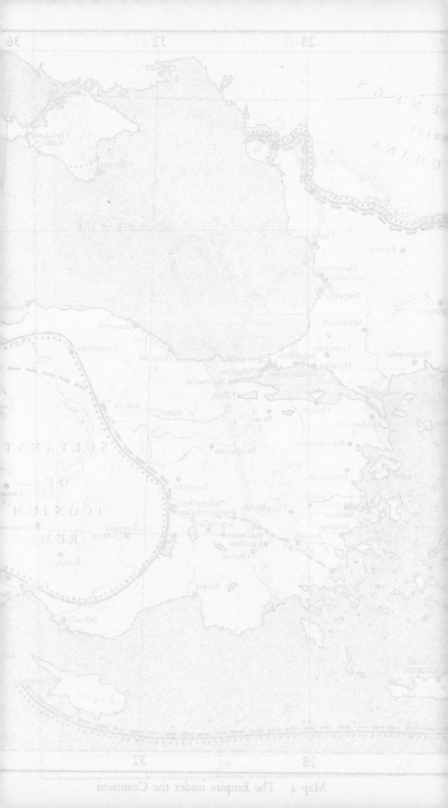

Map 4   The Empire under the Comneni

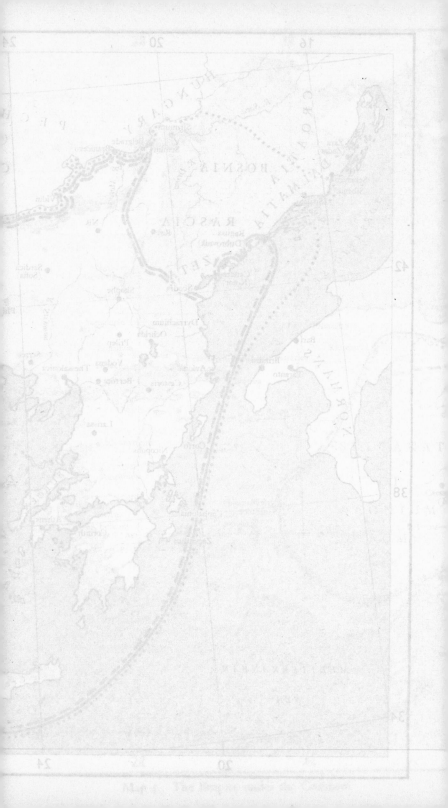

new threat with a kind of weary dignity. It was a time when Byzantine feelings about their Frankish and Seljuq neighbours were hardening. The border barons, Byzantine *akritai* and Seljuq ghazis and *uç beys*—marcher lords dedicated to Islam— got on tolerably well together; neither side cared much for the Turkomans who were not to be subdued until the late fifteenth century. With the Seljuqs, Anna shows Alexius as being gracious, but very firm:

'The Sultan (Malik Şah of Konya, 1107–16) had approached with all his subject satraps . . . and met the Emperor in the plain between Augustopolis and Acronium. When the satraps espied the Emperor from a distance they got off their horses and offered the obeisance usually made to Kings. The Sultan several times attempted to dismount, but the Emperor would not allow it, the other however jumped down quickly and kissed the Emperor's foot, who gave him his hand and begged him to mount one of the noblemen's horses. When he had mounted and was riding close to the Emperor's side, [Alexius] suddenly took off the cloak he was wearing and threw it round the Sultan's shoulders. After a short silence he made known to him all he had decided upon, saying, "If you are willing to submit to the [Byzantine] Empire and cease your onslaughts on the Christians, you shall enjoy favours and honour and live at peace for the rest of your life in the countries assigned to you, where you formerly had your dwellings before [the defeat at Manzikert]. And if you listen to my words, who am giving you wise counsel, you will never repent . . .; if you do not, then be assured that I shall be the destroyer of your race." '

Alexius, or rather Anna Comnena, was over-hopeful, but the atmosphere of the meeting is genuine enough. In early Turkish heroic poetry the Byzantines figure as wonderful neighbours, brave warriors and Amazon princesses. As in Byzantine and Armenian epic, which have the long wars with the caliphate as their background, there is a noticeable absence of any clash of cultures, Christian and Muslim. But, though they were

H

Christian, the new enemies from the West represented a very alien culture. Turkish emirs were one thing, but Frankish counts were a different sort of opponent altogether.

In the last years of the eleventh century the Normans consolidated two widely separated conquests: England and Sicily. From Sicily the rakish Norman warlord Robert Guiscard turned to pester the Balkan possessions of the Empire. So, when in 1096 the First Crusade was launched to capture Jerusalem and the Holy Sepulchre from Byzantium's Seljuq neighbours, and when Guiscard's son Bohemund turned up among the Crusade's leaders, Alexius had grave misgivings. He had reached a position of some confidence: in 1091 he had crushed the Patzinaks, for centuries Byzantium's northern threat. Alexius was slowly making ground in Anatolia and taking advantage of dissension among the Turks to play one against the other. Pope Urban II claimed that the Emperor had asked for a crusade against the infidel. That he had in fact asked, as on earlier occasions, for anything more than mercenaries, is inconceivable. The accident of a temporary vacuum of power in Anatolia and Syria allowed the First Crusaders to reach Jerusalem, but the insecure kingdom which they set up there was doomed to fall as soon as either Syria or Egypt got the upper hand over the other and required Palestine for itself. In the end the crusaders learned nothing and forgot nothing. But they were not entirely insignificant, for they served to bring Byzantines and Franks face to face in numbers for the first time. Alexius arranged the Frankish passage with great skill, but everyone's worst suspicions were confirmed. Anna Comnena described what happened:

'Before [Alexius] had enjoyed even a short rest, he heard a report of the approach of innumerable Frankish armies. Now he dreaded their arrival for he knew their irresistible manner of attack, their unstable and mobile character...; and he also knew that they were always agape for money, and seemed to disregard their truces readily for any reason that cropped up. . . . However, he did not lose heart, but prepared himself in every way so that, when the occasion called, he would be ready for battle. And indeed the actual facts were far greater and more terrible than rumour made them. For the whole of the West and all the barbarian tribes which dwell between the farther side of the Adriatic and the pillars of Hercules, had all migrated in a body and were marching into Asia through the intervening Europe. . . . The simpler-minded were urged on by a real desire of worshipping at Our Lord's Sepulchre, and visiting the sacred places; but the more astute, especially men like Bohemund . . . , had another secret motive. . . .

'By then the Emperor was engulfed in an immense sea of worries, for he had long grasped the fact that the Franks were dreaming of the [Byzantine] Empire itself. . . .'

This was Byzantium's first great encounter with the West. At Ochrida, Theophylact, the gentle and learned Greek Archbishop of Bulgaria, watched the barbarian crusaders pass through with mounting dismay. When they reached Constantinople Alexius arranged for the Frankish leaders to have access to him daily. They clattered about the palace. 'Now the Frankish Counts are naturally shameless and violent, immoderate in everything they wish, and possess a flow of language greater than any other human race. . . . They had no reverence for the Emperor, nor took heed of the lapse of time nor suspected the indignation of onlookers,' observed Anna. They pursued him to his bedchamber, but he would listen patiently into the small hours for 'he was afraid lest from some trifling pretext a great fire of scandal should be lighted and great harm ensue to the [Byzantine] Empire.'

Alexius let the Crusaders do the talking, but usually won the argument. He persuaded the counts to take oaths of fealty to restore to him those parts of the Empire which had been lost to the Seljuqs; from the beginning there was a clash of interests. But on both sides distaste was mingled with fascination, the profound mutual attraction of rivals. The Byzantines adopted

Western military tactics while the artists and scholars of Constantinople fed the twelfth-century Renaissance of Western Europe through mutual points of contact in Sicily, Venice and (now that the intervening Patzinaks had been reduced) Hungary. Manuel, Alexius' grandson, was particularly beguiled by the West, and by the chivalry and easy companionship of Frankish rulers. Such equivocal feelings date also from the First Crusade. In personal terms they are summed up by Anna's impression of Bohemund, later to be renegade prince of Byzantine Antioch:

'It must be confessed that there was something attractive about the man, though the effect was impaired by alarming qualities on all sides. For, as a whole he appeared as a beast of prey; where others laughed he roared like a lion. But he was so made, in mind and body, that ferocity and love were always rampant in him, each seeking vent in war...'

In the background of the Byzantine encounter with the West was the growing realisation, even among such generous-minded scholars as Theophylact of Ochrida, that the Universal Church had in fact lost its unity. Latins seemed to worship differently, but, perhaps more important, they ran their Church differently. Popes such as Gregory VII and Innocent III were making claims for Rome which did not agree with the Orthodox belief that authority is vested in the whole Church and in the Councils which had been inspired by the Holy Wisdom of God. It was unfortunate that, at this juncture, some Byzantine canon lawyers and Patriarchs temporarily evolved counter-claims for the supremacy of Constantinople. Legally, what was later to be called a schism occurred when the Crusaders elected rival Latin Patriarchs in Jerusalem (1099), Antioch (1100) and, eventually, Constantinople itself (1206). Probably Pope Urban II, and possibly Alexius himself, had in mind a formal Union of the Churches before the First Crusade, but it was the Crusade and, in particular, the determination of Bohemund to keep Byzantine Antioch for himself, which made it practically impossible.

The Orthodox Church was the peculiar and distinguishing mark of the Byzantine Empire and the Crusaders, rather than the Seljuqs, were putting its most precious tradition at stake. For the papacy it was a matter of discipline; for the Byzantines it threatened their very identity. Long before 1204 some Greeks were wondering if the turban of the Sultan was not preferable to the tiara of the Pope. Patriarch Michael III (1169–77) said as much to his pro-Western Emperor Manuel Comnenus:

'Let the Muslim be my master in outward things rather than the Latin dominate me in matters of the spirit. For if I am subject to the Muslim, at least he will not force me to share his faith. But if I have to be under the Frankish rule and united with the Roman Church, I may have to separate myself from my God.'

The motives of the papacy, the German rulers and of the crusaders were only intelligible to many Byzantines if they were sinister. Equally Franks regarded Greeks as alien, slippery and on terms with infidels such as Saladin which could only be called treacherous. Each regarded the other as a dangerous nuisance. It was a meeting between two peoples each with a superiority complex. The Franks stood low in the Byzantine view of a hierarchy of nations, but when by the 1180s these Westerners had actually proved their superiority, it was the Byzantine's turn to become noisily resentful and, in the tone of Nicetas Choniates' words, just a touch hysterical:

'Between us and the Latins is set the widest gulf. We are poles apart. We have not a thought in common. They are stiff-necked with a proud affectation of an upright carriage, and love to sneer at the smoothness and modesty of our manners. But we look upon their arrogance and boasting and pride as the snot which keeps their noses in the air; and we tread them down with the might of Christ, who giveth unto us the power to trample upon the adder and the scorpion.'

These Franks were a standing affront to the God-given order of things. This is why the Fourth Crusaders' sack of Constantinoble was so damaging to the Byzantine conception of the world.

By 1204 Byzantine disillusion with the West was widespread. Greeks could not help comparing Muslim and Latin methods of warfare, for instance the Norman sack of Thessalonica in 1185 by contrast with Saladin's capture of Jerusalem from the Crusaders two years later. 'The Muslims showed exemplary humanity and clemency,' observed Choniates, 'nor did they commit the atrocities which these professedly Christian co-religionists of ours committed against us without provocation.' The sack of Constantinople, the Queen City, by Western Crusaders left what was later to become the most appalling memory of all among Orthodox Byzantines. The Franks were equally impressed by the occasion. Constantinople, the most desirable and mysterious of medieval cities, offered irresistible plunder. It was the unworthy guardian of more Christian relics than had ever been found in the Holy Land; it was 'Constantinopolitana, civitas diu profana'. One Crusader describes how they entered the disheartened capital on April 13th, 1204:

'The booty gained was so great that none could tell you the end of it: gold and silver, and vessels and precious stones, and samite, and cloth of silk, and robes vair and grey, and ermine, and every choicest thing found upon the earth.

'Of the treasure that was found in the palace I cannot speak, for there was so much that it was beyond end or counting. Never, since the world was created, had so much been plundered in any city. So the host of pilgrims and Venetians praised the Lord, since they were no more than twenty thousand armed men, and they had vanquished four hundred thousand men, or more, and in the strongest city in all the world—yea, it was a great city.'

Villehardouin describes only half the reality. On the other side Nicholas Mesarites made it his business to see that the Byzantines never forgot the indignity:

'Then the streets, squares, two-storied and three-storied houses, holy places, convents, houses of monks and nuns, holy churches (even God's Great Church), the imperial palace, were filled with the enemy, all war-maddened swordsmen, breathing murder, iron-clad and spear-bearing, sword-bearers and lance-bearers, bowmen, horsemen, boasting, dreadfully, baying like Cerberus and breathing like Charon, pillaging the holy places, trampling on divine things, running riot over holy things, casting down to the floor the holy images of Christ and His holy Mother and of the holy men who from eternity have been pleasing to the Lord God, uttering calumnies and profanities, and in addition tearing children from mothers and mothers from children, treating the virgin with wanton shame in holy chapels, viewing with fear neither the wrath of God nor the vengeance of men. . . . They slaughtered the new-born, killed matrons, stripped elder women, and outraged old ladies; they tortured the monks, they hit them with their fists and kicked their bellies, thrashing and rending their reverend bodies with whips. . . . Such was the reverence for holy things of those who bore the Lord's Cross on their shoulders, thus their own bishops taught them to act. Then why call them bishops? Bishops among soldiers or soldiers among bishops?'

How had this disaster come about? In many ways it was a question of when, rather than how. The notion of a diversionary crusade to save the ailing Latin state in the Holy Land by attacking Egypt, or even Byzantium, was not new. German rulers, such as Conrad III, Frederick Barbarossa and Henry VI, had been looking covetously on the Eastern imperial capital for much of the twelfth century (for they too called themselves 'Emperor'), and the papacy had long entertained hopes of bringing the Greek church into the Roman fold. What was new was that this Crusade was the first which, because the

Balkan and Anatolian routes were finally closed, had to go by sea. Venice had the only navy capable of transporting such an expedition and hence the Crusaders were in Venetian hands from the beginning. There followed a chapter of accidents. But, once again, it was Byzantium that had really invited the disaster, and only partly was it a failure of diplomacy of the Angeli. The truth was that in the previous thirty years the Empire had been falling to pieces on its own account; the Fourth Crusade was only the culmination of an internal process. If the Westerners had not come in 1204 (or the Seljuqs in 1071), one wonders if things would have turned out very differently.

The thirty years which led up to 1204 are as crucial as the decades which preceded Manzikert in 1071. There were squabbles over the imperial throne; the new Angelus dynasty (1185–1204) produced no rulers to equal the Comneni. Indeed the Angeli have the distinction of having promoted more pretenders and impostors than legitimate Emperors. Independent feudatories detached whole provinces: Isaac Comnenus of Cyprus in 1184, Theodore Mankaphas of Philadelphia in 1188, Leon Sgouros of the Eastern Morea in 1189 and Alexius and David Comnenus of Trebizond a few days before Constantinople itself fell in 1204. Landowners were opting out of the state. Increasingly they failed to pass on the taxes they exacted to the imperial officials. Their serfs, now denied access to imperial courts, were becoming more desperate. Small wonder that the peasantry greeted the Byzantine nobility who fled from Constantinople in 1204 with nothing but derision.

The state and the Church, its representative and most efficient landowner of all, had to exploit their remaining resources beyond what they could endure, particularly in the southern Balkans. The unity of Greek society was broken; poets such as the semi-legendary Theodore 'Poor' Prodromus turned from eulogising the old Comnene dynasty to writing scurrilous ballads about the rich—who included, of course, the monks who now dominated the Church:

'To come now to the monks' food and what goes on at meal-
times, I couldn't possibly begin to tell it all in detail—how first
they sound the gong three times and all go rushing in, and
once the grace is duly said, they all set to and eat. A vast array
of fish is brought and set before the monks, some reserved for
anchorites, but Father Abbot grabs that—and his little boy-
friend gobbles up what's left. And while they gorge themselves
like this—what do they give me, but dry bread and dirty soup
on which they've chucked a blessing? My belly swells to think
of it, so let me say no more.'

Prodromus gives us a glimpse into a much wider unrest,
social, intellectual and moral. In these years Byzantium lost its
sense of direction. There was a curious indecision about Byzantine foreign policy. More than one Angelus Emperor would
not move until he had consulted a soothsayer—the gipsies
who reached the Empire from the East in the twelfth century had a particular vogue as fortune tellers at this time. In
1197 the Seljuq Sultan Süleyman II founded a colony in his
dominion for Byzantines who preferred Muslim security and
tax-exemptions to the uncertainties of their own Empire.
Choniates chronicles how Byzantines then, and earlier, had
found refuge among the Turks:

'Their intercourse with the Turks of Konya had resulted not
only in a firm mutual friendship, but in the adoption by the
Christians of the Turkish way of life in many respects, and they
were so friendly with their Turkish neighbours that they regarded the [Byzantines] as their enemies. Habit, ingrained by
passage of Time, is indeed stronger than race or religion.
'The truth was that in the [Byzantine] world, by our day,
the springs of Christian virtue had dried up, the truths [of
religion] had ceased to be taken seriously, and arbitrary injustice had run riot until the natural affections of the majority of
the population had been chilled to a degree at which entire
Hellenic communities voluntarily opted for finding new homes

among the barbarians and rejoiced to get away from their native land.'

With some justice, many Byzantines focused their resentment upon the merchant colonists of Italy as being the source of all their troubles. Venice, until quite recently a Byzantine city, had a special relationship with the Empire. Alexius I and his successors granted Venice trading concessions throughout the Empire, and other Italian cities—Pisa, Amalfi, Genoa—were soon claiming privileges also. The Italians brought to the bustling quays of Constantinople the *lingua franca* of Mediterranean sailors, introducing to Byzantine Greek much of its maritime—and obscene—vocabulary. But Byzantium lagged behind in shipbuilding techniques and business methods. Byzantine merchants, with their inefficient credit system and still hampered by high tariffs, could not compete with the privileged Italians. The aggressive prosperity of the Italian sovereign colonies in Byzantine cities led to considerable ill-feeling among Greeks who felt that their commerce had been abandoned to the West. In 1182 Andronicus, last of the Comnene Emperors, came to the throne on a wave of popular resentment against the West. In that year the Genoese and Pisans in Constantinople were massacred. Venice was already waiting for vengeance (and annual payments of compensation), for her merchants had been expelled or massacred in 1171. The Republic's day came in 1204 when, in the Fourth Crusade, Venice took the pick of the Empire. Henry Dandolo, its calculating blind old doge, proclaimed in his very title his share of the loot. He called himself 'Lord of a Quarter and of Half of a Quarter of the [Byzantine] Empire.'

While Byzantium was alienating the Italians and breaking up among its own feudatories, its enemies seized their opportunity. In 1176 the Seljuqs confirmed their conquests at the battle of Myriocephalum. In 1185 the Normans went on the rampage in captured Thessalonica. The non-Greek areas of the Balkans rose at last. By 1180 Serbia was virtually independent and Hungary had taken Dalmatia. Bulgaria and Wallachia rose a few years later. The Angeli fought back in Thrace, but the division of the Empire among its component peoples had been completed before 1204. By this process of elimination the Greeks, perhaps for the first time, became the majority people in Byzantium. But they were also the last to gain independence of their own Empire, just as the Turks were later to become the last to achieve national independence of the Ottoman Empire.

The Greeks never really came to terms with the loss of their imperial rôle, but the experiences of these years were already driving them to seek comfort once more in the still accumulating traditions of Hellenism and Orthodoxy. From the late XIIth century Greek writers were occasionally calling themselves 'Hellenes' rather than 'Romans', and now it was becoming increasingly obvious that the only 'Romans' left in the Empire were in fact 'Hellenes'. And Greek scholarship and art were particularly lively during the thirty years before 1204; from these decades the final, Palaeologan, revival traces its origins.

The loss of the capital in 1204 solved a number of problems for the Greeks, for after the initial shock they found that they had been more successful than they had dared hope. The puppet Latin Empire was never viable, but, by taking the brunt of the expansion of the new Bulgarian kingdom, served to shield the Greek states temporarily exiled from Constantinople. Venice already had most of what it wanted in Byzantium, and only aroused the hostility of Genoa, which became an ally of the Greek rulers. Pope Innocent III never won his Universal Church. The Crusading ideal was debased for ever; the Holy Land itself was forgotten and lost. But new life and a new confidence came to the surviving Greek provinces. In the troubles which preceded the Seljuq conquest of 1071–81 and in the internal disintegration which made Constantinople defenceless in 1204, Byzantium lost most of those features which marked it out from any other European feudal state, but found a final identity. Byzantium entered the late medieval world, not as a Universal Empire, but as what looked very like a national state.

BIBLIOGRAPHY

Two of the finest sources for the period are available in translation and both recently reprinted:

Dawes, E. A. (trans.), *The Alexiad of Anna Comnena: being the History of the reign of her father, Alexius I, Emperor of the Romans 1081–1118*. Routledge, 1928 (1967).

Sewter, E. R. A. (trans.), *The Chronographia of Michael Psellus*. Routledge, 1953 (1966).

Other important books for the period are:

Brand, C. M., *Byzantium confronts the West, 1180–1204*. Harvard U.P., 1968.

Chalandon, F., *Les Comnène*. Paris, 1900–1912.

Frolow, A., *Recherches sur la déviation de la IVe Croisade vers Constantinople*. Paris, 1955.

Hussey, J. M., *Church and Learning in the Byzantine Empire 867–1185*. Oxford U.P., 1937.

Laurent, J., *Byzance et les Tures Seljoucides dans l'Asia Occidentale jusqu' en 1081*. Paris, 1913.

Ostrogorsky, G., *Pour l'histoire de la féodalité Byzantine* and *Quelques problèmes de l'Histoire de la paysannerie Byzantine*. Brussels, 1954 and 1956.

Runciman, S., *The Eastern Schism*. Oxford U.P., 1955.

Setton, K. M., *A History of the Crusades*. Two volumes. Pennsylvania U.P., 1955 and 1962.

Svoronos, N., *Société et organisation intérieur dans l'Empire ...*: In *Proceedings of the XIIth International Congress of Byzantine Studies*. Oxford U.P., 1967.

Vryonis, S., *Byzantium, the social basis of the decline in the XIth century*, In *Greek, Roman and Byzantine Studies*, vol. II. Cambridge, Mass., 1959.

VI

The Second Encounter with the West:
A.D. 1204-1453

JOSEPH GILL, S.J.

The capture of Constantinople in 1204 by the Fourth Crusade disrupted the Christian East. The Greeks lost their capital city with all the area around, and all the peninsula of Greece, but they did not surrender. They set up three separate kingdoms; one in Trebizond was already just in being as a result of a revolt against the Angeli in 1204, and there were added one based on Nicaea and another in Epirus. Of these the Kingdom of Nicaea was the most important, because Theodore Lascaris, son-in-law of the dead Emperor Alexius III, assumed power there, and very soon it became also the place of residence of the Greek Patriarch.

The Latin victors divided up the conquered territory in feudal fashion among themselves. Venice received three-eighths of the city of Constantinople itself, and the best ports on the newly acquired seaboard. The new Latin Emperor was Baldwin, Count of Flanders. Besides sovereignty over only five-eighths of his own Constantinople, he received territory carefully calculated so that he should not be strong enough to dominate the other Latin kingdoms, with the result that his Empire was actually too weak to be stable.

The crusaders had captured Constantinople: they had still to conquer the Empire. Baldwin drove east to establish his claims over Greek Asia Minor and Lascaris had to retire before him. Boniface of Montferrat, to whom Thessalonica had been allotted, went south and without too much difficulty made himself lord of most of the eastern plains of continental Greece and the Morea. The Bulgarians, however, rejected as allies, became enemies. Baldwin hastened back to meet them, but was captured and never heard of again. Dandolo the aged Venetian

Doge died, and in 1207 Boniface was killed in a skirmish with the Bulgarians. The three leading personalities of the Latin Empire had vanished from the scene within three years. The Bulgarian campaign gave a respite to Lascaris to consolidate. He was crowned Emperor by the new Greek Patriarch of Constantinople in Nicaea in 1208. Likewise the ruler of the Despotate of Epirus on the western Greek seaboard, Michael Ducas, used the occasion by pacts with the Venetians and the Latins (which he broke on the first convenient occasion), to render Epirus independent and a rival to Nicaea.

The rest of the history of the Latin Empire of Constantinople is the story of rivalry between Nicaea and Epirus for hegemony of the Greeks and possession of Constantinople, of Bulgarian intrigues with now one and now the other and its own aspirations to the Byzantine imperial throne, and of Latin resistance on a diminishing scale. Henry of Flanders, who succeeded Baldwin I, was the best of the Latin Emperors. A fine soldier, moderate in his relations with others, tolerant, he gave stability to his Empire internally by repressing a revolt of the barons of Thessaly and externally by defeating Lascaris, and he gained the respect also of the Greeks. Yet even he had to make a treaty with Lascaris at Nymphaeum, which implied a recognition of a Nicaean kingdom. He died prematurely at the age of forty in 1216. His successor was ambushed on his way to Constantinople by Theodore Ducas of Epirus and disappeared. A regency for a minor, followed by a weak Emperor in Robert of Courtenay, while in Nicaea the redoubtable John Ducas Vatatzes followed Theodore Lascaris in 1222, resulted in the Latins being thrust out of Asia Minor.

By 1225 the Emperor governed little more than Constantinople and its suburbs. Theodore Ducas of Epirus had himself crowned Emperor in Thessalonica in 1225, but was checked by Bulgaria (1230). Bulgaria and Nicaea combined to attack Constantinople in 1235 and again in 1236, but the stout fortifications and the bravery of the defenders thwarted the attempts.

Only the rivalry among its enemies and the diversion of a

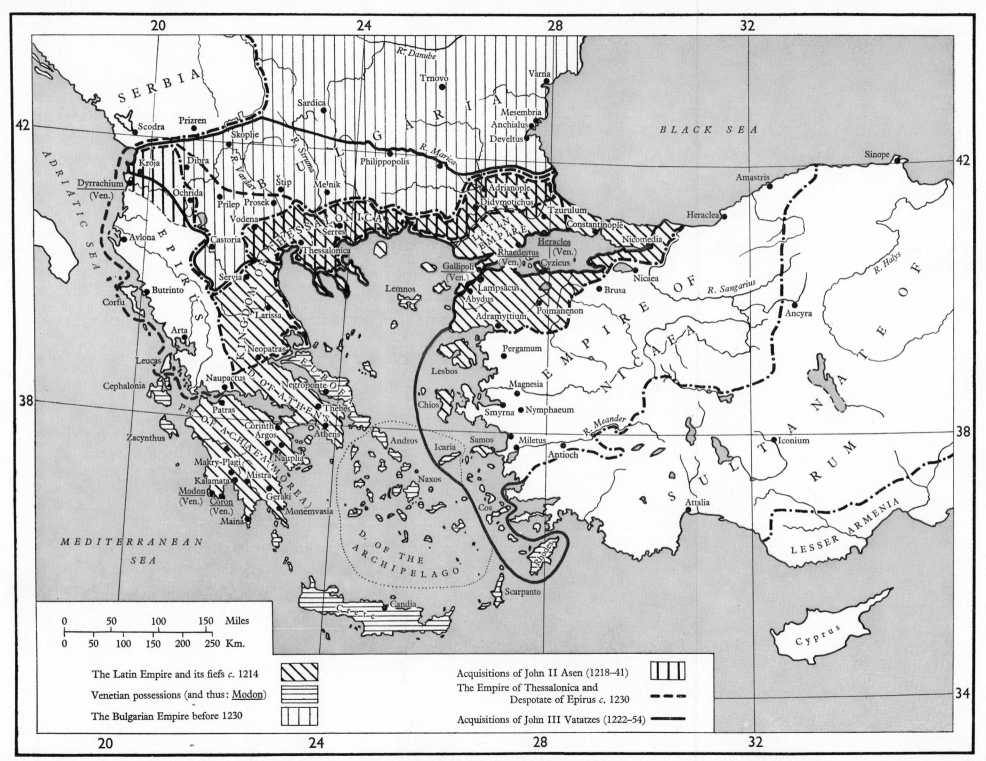

Map 5 The Age of Latin rule in Constantinople

Legend:

The Latin Empire and its fiefs *c.* 1214

Venetian possessions (and thus: Modon)

The Bulgarian Empire before 1230

Acquisitions of John II Asen (1218–41)

The Empire of Thessalonica and
Despotate of Epirus *c.* 1230

Acquisitions of John III Vatatzes (1222–54)

Mongolian threat to their flanks prolonged the existence of the
Latin Empire. Vatatzes employed also the arms of diplomacy.
He was on terms of friendship with Frederick II of Germany,
to whose illegitimate daughter he was married, and he negotiated with Pope Innocent IV about Church union, promising
recognition of a Roman primacy (and the Church seemed
strangely in accord with him) in return for a Greek Emperor
and a Greek Patriarch in Constantinople, and no Latin.
Vatatzes and Innocent both died in 1254. His successor at
Nicaea was less capable and in any case died in 1258 leaving
an heir only eight years old. An ambitious and effective general,
Michael Palaeologus, whose loyalty in the past had been twice
challenged, got himself made regent, then co-Emperor. By a
mixture of fine generalship and treachery the Latin forces of
Greece with those of the Despotate of Epirus were crushingly
defeated at Pelagonia in 1259. In 1261 an expedition near
Constantinople found the city undefended and took possession.
Michael hastened to the capital, had himself crowned sole-Em-
peror and blinded his young rival, who disappeared from history.

The Pope at the time of the capture of Constantinople was
Innocent III. He had been appalled when he heard of the sack-
ing of the eastern capital by crusaders pledged to fight the
infidel, not their fellow Christians. In his reaction he expressed
his anger in no uncertain terms.

'... How can we expect the Greek Church, no matter what
straits it is in, to return to ecclesiastical unity and devotion to
the Holy See when all that it sees of the Latins is an example of
utter depravity and of the works of darkness, so that with
justice it despises them as worse than dogs. Those defenders of
Christ have drenched their swords, which they should have
wielded against the pagans, in Christian blood. They have re-
spected neither religion, nor age, nor sex.... They have committed in open day adultery, fornication and incest. Matrons
and virgins, even those vowed to God, were delivered to the
ignominious brutality of the soldiery. And it was not enough

I

for them to squander the treasures of the Empire and to rob private individuals, whether great or small. They have dared to lay their hands on the wealth of the churches. They have been seen tearing from the altars the silver ornaments, breaking them in fragments over which they quarrelled, violating the sanctuaries, carrying away the icons, crosses and relics. . . .'[1]

Innocent III had always desired to promote the union of the Greek and Latin Churches. The new situation, unfortunate in its origin, gave him nevertheless a fortunate chance of achieving what he desired, for now most of the patriarchate of Constantinople was in Latin hands. To use the occasion to the full, he would have had to have been not merely years, but centuries in advance of his time. He was not. He was very much in the stream of current Latin thinking that then made the Pope the supreme spiritual power and indeed also the arbiter of political power. From the Greeks he—and after him his successors—demanded an oath of obedience to the Holy See, which most of them would not give. He believed that they were guilty of a variety of errors in doctrine and he judged the Greek liturgical rite inferior to the Latin, but apart from insisting on anointings did not try to change it. For their part, the Greeks harboured similar views about the Latin Church.

Innocent did his best to protect ecclesiastical property against the rapacity of the crusaders. He imposed submission to the Holy See on the new Latin Patriarch of Constantinople and sent Legates Apostolic to effect unity. Neither the conciliatory attitude of the first of these nor the harsher methods of the second were effective. The Greek Church rallied round the Patriarch in Nicaea, and most of the leading prelates abandoned their Sees to live there. To the Fourth Council of the Lateran (1215) Innocent invited only those bishops who had taken the oath of obedience, which meant that it was a Latin gathering. The Council, while not allowing two bishops in any one diocese, even though of different rite, legislated for at least an oriental 'vicar general' if the bishop was Latin. In the next

council (of Lyons, 1245) Innocent IV called the Latin Kingdom of Constantinople 'one of the five wounds that afflicted
him', and referred to it no more, probably judging its case
hopeless. It was he, however, who negotiated with Vatatzes,
receiving and sending several embassies. But he dare not affront
public opinion in the West by jettisoning the Latin Empire in
favour of Nicaea and he would not accept a union that left the
fundamental dogmatic difference of the *Filioque* unresolved.
The successors of both Pope Innocent and Emperor Vatatzes
continued the negotiations. In 1256 papal legates met the
Emperor Theodore, the Greek Patriarch and some thirty prelates in Thessalonica, but the conversations did not bring union
and were not renewed before the Greeks gained what they
wanted—political and ecclesiastical possession of Constantinople in 1261. So after nearly sixty years, when the Latin
kingdom of Constantinople came to an end, the old ecclesiastical breach was still unbridged.

The Greeks regained Constantinople in 1261, and the new
Emperor was Michael VIII of the family of Palaeologus from
Nicaea. The fugitive Latin Emperor appealed to the West for
help to regain his throne, and first Manfred of Sicily, then his
successor, Charles of Anjou, were ready allies, for they coveted
the throne of Constantinople for themselves. To restrain them
Michael turned to the Holy See with a suggestion of Church
union. Pope Urban IV replied cautiously but positively, for
besides wishing to end the ecclesiastical schism he was also
anxious to check the ambitions of a too powerful neighbour.
His successor Clement IV went a step further: he sent the
Emperor Michael for his acceptance, a profession of faith. This
contained not only the many dogmas that were common to
both Churches, but also some that were not—the papal head-
ship of the whole Church and the *Filioque* doctrine; that is,
that within the Blessed Trinity the Holy Spirit proceeds from
the Son as well as from the Father. These were the two main
points at issue between the Greek and Latin Churches.

On Clement's death, Gregory X was elected Pope. As Pope

he held three purposes dear: the freeing of the Holy Land, Church reunion, and Church reform. In all three he was intensely sincere. To implement his aims, he summoned a general council of the Church at Lyons, to which he invited the Emperor, Michael VIII, and the Patriarch of Constantinople, Joseph I.

Michael had every reason for accepting the Pope's invitation, for Charles of Anjou was rapidly preparing to attack. But first he had to win the approval of the Greek Church. At a preliminary meeting of the bishops he failed, largely through the opposition of the prominent deacon John Beccus, whom he therefore imprisoned, and of the Patriarch Joseph, who was then persuaded to go into temporary retirement. Finally, partly by persuasion, partly by threats, he prevailed on some forty-two metropolitans to sign a letter addressed to the Pope. Thereupon Michael himself solemnly made the profession of faith proposed by Pope Clement, and Andronicus, his son and fellow emperor, associated himself with his father's act. The Greek deputation therefore, could now set off for the Council at Lyons. It was small. Another ex-Patriarch Germanus and one of the highest court-officials, the Grand Logothete, George Akropolites, represented the Emperor; to represent the Church of the Greeks there was only Theophanes, metropolitan of Nicaea, for his companion-envoy had died on the eve of the voyage. The imperial legation did not reach Lyons until June 24th 1274, when the Council, which had begun on May 7th, had already completed its third session.

A few days later the feast of Saints Peter and Paul was celebrated. During the pontifical mass, the epistle, the gospel and the creed were chanted in both Latin and Greek. In the creed, sung by Greek delegates along with others who knew the language, not only was the *Filioque* sung, but it was sung twice. This was generally interpreted as a declaration of union and great was the rejoicing. The formal proclamation came a few days later. In the fourth session of the council on July 6th the letters of the Emperor and the bishops were read out in a

Latin translation, and Akropolites took an oath, in his master's name, of submission to the Pope and the Western Church. Michael's profession of faith was complete and unconditional; not so that of the bishops. The following two passages from the letters read out in the council deal with the same point and illustrate the difference of attitude. The first is from the Emperor's letter.

'... The holy Roman Church possesses supreme and full primacy and governance over the universal Catholic Church, which she truly and humbly recognises that she has received with the plenitude of power from the Lord Himself in the person of St. Peter, prince or head of the Apostles, whose successor is the Roman Pontiff. And just as among her other obligations she must defend the truth of the faith, so if doubts about the faith arise, they must be defined by her judgement. Anyone troubled with questions that pertain to the ecclesiastical forum can appeal to her and can have recourse to her judgement in all legal cases needing ecclesiastical examination. To that same Church all other Churches are subject and their prelates owe obedience and reverence....'

The Greek metropolitans committed themselves less definitely.

'... God-honoured pontiff, we prelates who are under the patriarchal See of Constantinople, together with the venerable clerics of our curias, make this proposal to you. From this short account you may conclude that, if only Your Magnitude will piously accept the legation's message, we both bow in acceptance of whatever you say and yield to the magnitude of Your Highness, and with great pleasure we offer whatever belongs to a total spiritual submission and refuse nothing of what our fathers before the schism gave to those who ruled the Apostolic See....'[2]

After such open adherence to the Latin faith on the part of the Emperor and the seeming acquiescence of the Eastern Church it is not to be wondered at that in the sixth and final session the *Filioque* clause, that is, the Procession of the Holy Spirit also from the Son, was defined as an article of faith. Union between the Eastern and Western Churches was now officially consummated, at least in Latin eyes.

The Greeks would claim, not unjustly, that it had been their Emperor not their Church that had accepted the Latin faith. All the same, the Emperor Michael did his best to make it accept. The Patriarch Joseph abdicated. John Beccus, led to acknowledge the orthodoxy of the *Filioque* by reading the ancient Fathers, was made the new patriarch.

The ex-patriarch Joseph, in spite of himself, became the centre of an opposition which grew rapidly and included higher clergy, most of the monks, of whom there were many, and lay folk from every grade of society. Even members of the Emperor's own family vehemently opposed him and did all they could to thwart his plans. Michael tried persuasion and, when persuasion failed, force. He imprisoned, exiled and mutilated leaders from among the non-unionists; but all in vain. Pachymeres, a Greek chronicler, describes how the Emperor tried to convince some papal envoys of the sincerity of his efforts.

'. . . The Emperor Michael Palaeologus knew that the chief purpose of the papal envoys was to insist that the peace between the Churches was not only an affair of words but also of deeds —deeds that would manifest that both parties held the same faith and so would implement the union. The envoys said that they were forced to adopt this attitude since the Greeks, though divided among themselves, had told them that the peace was a farce and that it should be put to the proof by whether they recited the creed like the Latins. To show them that the peace was not a farce, the Emperor bade Isaac, bishop of Ephesus, conduct the papal envoys to the public prison for them to see members of his own imperial family confined there because they had refused to accept the peace. They were heavily chained in the four corners of a square cell. . . .'[3]

Meanwhile Michael pursued his aim of reconquering all the

territory lost by the Fourth Crusade. He engaged in campaigns against the Greek princedoms of Epirus and Thessaly, not always successfully, but inflicted some telling defeats on Angevin forces operating in Albania and Greece. His fleet destroyed a naval force of the Latin lords of the Archipelago at Demetrias in 1275 and captured most of the islands including the large Venetian possession of Negroponte (Euboea). Venice quickly made a treaty with him. A crushing defeat of a powerful expedition launched by Anjou to prepare the way for his long-heralded attack on Constantinople was achieved at Berat (1280–81). For their part the popes had been becoming more and more insistent on some tangible evidence of the union from the side of the clergy of the Empire and many were the embassies and letters exchanged. Finally, Pope Martin IV, a Frenchman and supporter of Charles of Anjou, sceptical of Michael's sincerity, excommunicated him on November 18th, 1281. Some four months later, on March 29th, 1282, Sicily revolted against Anjou in what is called *The Sicilian Vespers*, and Charles, now King only of Naples, was incapable of further offensive action against Byzantium. The Emperor Michael was saved politically, but he was excommunicated again by Martin IV and died on December 11th, 1282. Execrated by the Oriental Church and excommunicated by the Roman, he was denied Christian burial.

With Michael's death all pretence at union was abandoned. His son Andronicus repudiated his part in it. Beccus was deposed. The Patriarch Joseph returned. The anti-unionists had their revenge and behaved as cruelly to the unionists as Michael had done to them. Beccus, condemned and banished, could have bought pardon and a career by recanting. Though three times interrogated at intervals, he refused and died in exile, a prisoner in a frontier castle.

The next century both in West and East was disastrous. In the West the popes were soon to take up residence in Avignon where they remained from 1309 till 1377. There was occasional talk of crusades—this time against Constantinople. The

Greek Emperors kept to themselves till they wanted protection either from the threat of a Latin crusade or from the incursions of the Turks. Then they applied to the pope of the West with words of union and the suggestion of a council, to receive the inevitable reply—implement the existing union first and then help will be forthcoming.

Politically the Byzantine Empire was in a bad way. The military schemes of Michael VIII to reconquer Greece, though successful for their immediate objects, had had a disastrous double effect. Carried out for the most part by mercenary armies, they had left the exchequer nearly bankrupt and they had diverted the energies of the Empire to the West, leaving the eastern frontiers inadequately protected against the advance of the Turks. By about the year 1300 Asia Minor, once the core of Byzantium, was lost to the Empire for ever, with the exception of a few fortresses and ports. Andronicus II, in an attempt to stem the Turkish tide, in 1303 invited in the Catalan or Grand Company, mercenaries some 6,500 strong, which fought successfully against the Turk. But then it turned to ravaging Byzantine territory and, when its captain had been murdered in the palace of Andronicus's eldest son Michael IX, it defeated the Greek army (1305), pillaged Thrace and, when there was no more left to destroy there, moved on to Thessaly. Greece was then in the hands of local lords, Greek and French. The Grand Company defeated them one by one till it settled in Athens (1311) where it remained for nearly eighty years.

The departure of the Catalan Grand Company from Thrace was a relief to Byzantium, but it did not free it from internal wars. The heir to the throne of Andronicus II, Andronicus III, the son of Michael IX who had died, exploited the dissatisfaction caused by his grandfather's imposition of new (and useful) taxes, to raise Thrace and Macedonia against the control of the central government. Helped by a wealthy young magnate, John Cantacuzenus, he forced the old man to divide the Empire with him (1321). There was war again in 1322 and Andronicus III was crowned co-Emperor. In 1328 the old Emperor was made to abdicate, and the grandson ruled alone over an impoverished realm which could not resist the attacks of its powerful neighbours, first the Bulgarians and then the Serbs. When Andronicus died in 1341, his heir, John V, was only ten years old. Rivalry for the power of regency between the dowager Empress Anne of Savoy and Cantacuzenus led to new civil wars. Cantacuzenus had himself proclaimed co-emperor in 1341, was crowned in 1346 first in Didymotichus and then in Constantinople, made himself sole Emperor in 1354, but in the same year he had to abdicate and retire to a monastery. John V with the help of Genoese and Serbs had triumphed over Cantacuzenus and his Turkish allies. The country had been devastated and the social distress had led to Thessalonica trying to make itself independent.

The Empire's neighbours were not slow to take advantage of the favourable opportunity offered them by the constant civil wars. King Stephen Dushan of Serbia, whose help was sought separately by both Cantacuzenus and the party of John V, let the rivals fight between themselves, while he annexed all Macedonia and in 1346 had himself crowned 'Emperor of the Serbs and the Greeks'. Since the early fourteenth century the Turks had been absorbing Asia Minor. In 1329 they had captured Nicaea; in 1337 Nicomedia. Through the short-sighted policy of Cantacuzenus these Turks were invited into Europe to help him against John V. By 1354 they were masters of the key-point, Gallipoli, and within eleven more years of rapid conquest in the Balkans had transferred their capital to Adrianople, to the north-west of Constantinople.

Other powers that benefited by the civil anarchy were the Italian city-states of Venice and Genoa. Each allied itself with one or other of the rival parties in the Byzantine civil wars in return for commercial privileges and always on opposite sides. Both had acquired many places of high commercial value. Venice held ports on both the east and west coasts of the Morea, Crete, Negroponte and various islands in the Aegean. Genoa had occupied Chios and other islands. Between them they practically controlled the trade of the eastern Mediterranean, and Constantinople itself, the geographical key to the granaries round the Black Sea, actually depended for its food on the shipping they provided. Genoa had its own little city of Pera across the Golden Horn; Venice its 'quarter' of Constantinople. Both enjoyed such enormous privileges and exemptions that they paid less custom-dues and taxes than the local Greek merchants.

The religious atmosphere of Constantinople in the first quarter of the XIVth century was so anti-Latin that the Emperor Andronicus III feared assassination if it should become known that he was communicating with the Holy See, and a secret messenger of his told the Pope: 'What separates the Greeks from you is not so much the difference of dogmas as the hatred they feel against the Latins, provoked by the wrongs they have suffered.' The atmosphere lightened with the accession of John V, whose mother, Anne of Savoy, had been a Latin. Clouds gathered again very shortly, owing to a controversy about a method of contemplative prayer practised by the monks of Mount Athos. Barlaam, an Orthodox monk from Calabria, but educated in the Latin environment of Padua, attacked it with ridicule. Gregory Palamas, one of the monks, defended it. The protagonists soon found partisans, produced treaties and counter-treaties, and gained political patrons. The Emperor's rival, Cantacuzenus, supported Palamas; John's party, Barlaam. In the end, in 1351, Palamas prevailed and his teaching became a test of orthodoxy. His opponents were dubbed 'Latin-minded' and subjected to persecution, although the controversy had been a purely internal dispute within the Greek Church.

Intermittently relations were re-established with the papal court with pleas for help. Andronicus II communicated three times with Avignon, but his envoys were Venetians and the Calabrian monk Barlaam, not Greeks. He was invited by the Pope to collaborate in a Naval League with Rhodes, France and Venice to put down the piracy based on Africa and particularly on the ports of Asia Minor that preyed on the commerce of the eastern Mediterranean. The Naval League was revived later and achieved some success in 1344 when it took Smyrna, the chief port of Omur Bey the ally of Cantacuzenus, and in 1347 off Imbros. Cantacuzenus, thereupon, sent messengers to the Pope to talk of Church Union (1348). The Pope replied by urging Genoa, Rhodes and Cyprus to protect Constantinople. He received, however, his next message, not from Cantacuzenus who had already abdicated, but from John V. The new Emperor offered his personal submission to the Roman Church and a variety of measures that he claimed would result shortly in genuine Church union, in return for immediate military help against the ever growing menace from the Turk. In answer, the Naval League was directed to Constantinopolitan waters as a protection, but more the Pope could not do, for he had no army and with England at war with France, Genoa and Venice the bitterest of rivals, and Germany divided, he could not raise a viable crusade. In 1369 John V, after a fruitless journey to the court of Hungary for assistance, went to Rome and made his submission. But it was no use. The Greek position: 'Council first, then union', and the Latin reply: 'Union first, then help, but no council', only played into Turkish hands.

On his way home from Rome, John V was held a year virtually a prisoner for debt in Venice, because his son and heir, Andronicus IV, refused to hand over the island of Tenedos to the Venetians, since his friends, the Genoese, wanted it. John V reached Constantinople in October 1371, a month after the crushing defeat of the Serbs at the river Marica by the Turks. John had to become a tribute-paying vassal of the Sultan for self-protection. Andronicus rebelled against his father in 1373 but was defeated. With Genoese help in 1376 he imprisoned both his father and his brother, Manuel, and in a mistaken act of friendship ceded Gallipoli to the Turks. The Venetians helped John to escape and with Turkish aid he regained his throne (1379). In 1390 he was temporally dethroned again and died in 1391. Manuel II succeeded him.

The Greek Empire, strangely enough, in its last years had more stability in the Peloponnesus than on the mainland. Emperor John Cantacuzenus sent his son, Manuel, to govern there in 1348 and till 1383 members of the Cantacuzenus family by, on the whole, wise administration helped the country regain some prosperity, by keeping the local barons at peace, introducing new inhabitants, and building up the centre of government in the town of Mistra. After 1383 sons of the Palaeologan emperors ruled. They managed to conquer all the peninsula except for the Venetian areas round Modon and Coron in the west and Nauplion and Argos in the east. In 1415 Manuel II built the wall 'Hexamilion' across the isthmus of Corinth but it could not resist the Sultan, Murad II, in 1423 and, rebuilt by Constantine XI Palaeologus in 1444, was overrun again in 1446. The Greeks retained the Peloponnesus during all those years as tribute-paying vassals of the Sultans and as such survived the fall of Constantinople till 1460 when the unnecessary and destructive wars between the Palaeologan brothers themselves made Mehmet II lose patience and turn them out.

The tragedy of eastern Europe in the fourteenth century was its division. Byzantium dissipated its waning strength by almost continuous civil wars. Byzantium, Serbia and Bulgaria each sought its own immediate advantage in the disasters of the others, instead of offering a united front to the all-devouring Turks, who in consequence crushed them one by one—in 1389 the Serbian Empire, in 1393 the Bulgarian, in 1396 the small western force of French and Hungarians, the so-called Crusade of Nicopolis sent to the defence of Constantinople. From 1394 till 1402 Constantinople was besieged and its reprieve came, not by force of Christian arms, but because the Mongol Timurlane defeated and captured the Ottoman Sultan. Meanwhile, the Greek Emperor, Manuel II, was touring the courts of Europe seeking help: from England he received £2,000 between 1399 and 1401. From that time on, contacts multiplied, for Italy, already immersed in a revival of Latin classical studies,

was now turning its enquiring mind to the Greek classics. In
1396 Florence invited the Greek, Manuel Chrysoloras, to teach
Greek in its university; soon Italians were going to Constantinople to learn Greek.

There, in spite of the upheavals that starred thirteenth-
century Byzantine history, the pursuit of learning continued.
The Emperors of Nicaea founded schools to preserve the
old tradition and Michael VIII on regaining Constantinople
did the same. A continuous line of historians has recounted in
detail the events recorded in this chapter—George Acropolites
(1217–82), politician and scholar; George Pachymeres (1242–
1310); Nicephorus Gregoras (1295–1359) who wrote copiously
also against Palamism; the Emperor John Cantacuzenus (c.
1292–1383) in his retirement in a monastery; George Sphrantzes (1401–78) and Laonicus Chalcocondyles (1432–90). Most
of them were men of letters as well as chroniclers. For example,
Acropolites, the pupil of Nicephorus Blemmydes, head of the
school in Nicaea, was given charge of the school founded in
Constantinople. Gregoras left behind him a collection of letters
which, like those of Demetrius Cydones (1324–97), Michael
Calecas (1410) and the Emperor Manuel II, are historical
documents as well as studied rhetorical exercises; a pupil of
the philosopher-statesman Theodore Metochites (1260–1332),
he wrote also on philosophy and inspired his more famous
pupil, George Gemistus Pletho, who at the end of the fourteenth and in the early fifteenth century in Mistra taught
a kind of neo-Platonism to many of the intellectuals of the day.
Gennadius, as Patriarch, destroyed Pletho's most important
work, *The Laws*, as being pagan and anti-Christian. In the last
decades of the waning life of the Byzantine Empire the schools
of Constantinople could not rival the imperial university and
the patriarchal school of previous centuries, but schools there
were that produced a new flowering of humanists whose interests lay in philosophy and, in view of relations with the Western Church, also in theology. Joseph Bryennius, the brothers
Eugenicus, Bessarion, Isidore of Kiev, and particularly George

Scholarius (later the Patriarch Gennadius) have left a mass of works, mainly controversial, written in the court classical Greek that often combines much grace with grammatical perfection. Scholarius also translated many works of St. Thomas Aquinas, whom he greatly admired as an acute commentator on Aristotle.

In the first two decades of the fifteenth century, while Constantinople enjoyed some respite from Turkish pressure, the Latin Church was involved in internal schism with two, and for a time three rival 'popes'. It solved its own problem of unity by a general council and then thought to end the Greek schism by the same means. At the Council of Constance (1414–18), which elected Martin V as Pope, there were representatives of the Emperor Manuel, who painted so rosy a picture of Greek readiness for union that Pope Martin immediately appointed a legate to effect it. But during his lifetime it did not get beyond the stage of negotiations, because Manuel followed the advice that he gave to his son, the future Emperor. The chronicler, Sphrantzes, reports it in these words:

'. . . My son, really and truly we know the Turk thoroughly well. He hesitates a great deal for fear that we should come to an agreement with the western Christians. For he believes that, if this should happen, he will suffer a great disaster at the hands of the Westerners, and all because of us. So, when you need to intimidate the Turk, raise the question of a council and make a demand for one, but never, never try to hold one in actual fact. As I see our people, they are never likely to devise a method and means of union that does not involve the return of the Westerners to our Church. But that is absolutely impossible; so much so that I really believe that the division between us would become worse and in that case we should be left completely isolated at the mercy of the Turk. . . .' [4]

The Turkish menace was never relaxed: it only varied in intensity. In 1422 the Sultan besieged Constantinople, but a revolt in Asia Minor led him to raise the siege. John VIII, then co-Emperor, travelled to the court of Hungary to seek help, but Sigismund was too involved in stabilising his own affairs to be able to assist. Manuel died in 1425. The Latins kept urging a common council to bring union between the Churches. John finally, despite his father's advice, decided to accept. Arrangements were on the point of being made when Martin V died in 1431. Negotiations followed with the Council of Basel and Eugenius IV. In 1437 the Pope implemented the agreement made between Basel and the imperial envoys. In consequence in February 1438 the Emperor arrived at the Pope's council in Ferrara with the Patriarch of Constantinople Joseph II, plenipotentiaries of the other three Orthodox patriarchs, a score of metropolitans and a host of clerics and courtiers, altogether about seven hundred persons, to form the most representative of all councils held so far.

The discussions got off to a slow start, for the Emperor insisted on a four months' wait to let the western princes arrive, from whom he hoped to obtain military aid to bolster up his Empire. When they did start, there was no agreement. Some six sessions about Purgatory left the parties as divided as before. The fourteen sessions on the legitimacy of adding to the creed brought no desired result. By that time it was December 1438, and the Greeks, already more than a year away from home, were depressed. Worse was to come. The council was transferred to Florence, because the papal exchequer, drained by the expenses of the Greeks' voyage and of their upkeep in Ferrara, was nearly empty and Florence offered loans on better terms.

The sessions began again in February 1439, this time on the doctrine of the *Filioque*, to try to decide which was right, the Greek formula: 'The Holy Spirit proceeds from the Father *through* the Son' or the Latin: 'The Holy Spirit proceeds from the Father *and* the Son.' There were eight sessions and still no agreement, and the Greeks wanted to go home. Then, surprisingly, unity came. Among the Greeks a party of the more intellectual prelates had been convinced for some time of the orthodoxy of the Latin doctrine. Now they urged their fellows that the saints do not err in the faith, yet each of the two Churches could boast of a long line of saints, the Greek ones saying 'through the Son', the Latin ones 'from the Son'. Both phrases then must be acceptable, if interpreted aright. The Greek synod was convinced and freely gave its assent.

In this way the basic theological difference dividing the Churches was solved. When two or three other points had, though with some difficulty, been agreed upon and the form of a decree mutually approved, on July 6th, 1439 in the cathedral church of Florence, union of the Churches of East and West was joyfully announced and greeted in Latin and Greek with 'Agreed'. Only two of the Greek prelates did not sign. The solution found at Florence was the same as that proposed by Beccus some 150 years earlier: that the doctrines of the two churches were equally orthodox. It was expressed in the decree of union in these words.

'... In the name then, of the Blessed Trinity, Father, Son and Holy Spirit, with the approval of this sacred general Council of Florence, we define that this truth of the faith should be believed and held by all Christians and thus that all should profess that the Holy Spirit is eternally from Father and Son and has his essence and subsistence at once from Father and Son and that He proceeds eternally from both as from one principle, declaring that what the holy doctors and Fathers of the Church say, namely, that the Holy Spirit proceeds from the Father *through* the Son, has this meaning, that by it is intended that the Son too is the cause, according to the Greeks, and according to the Latins the principle, of the subsistence of the Holy Spirit, just as is the Father. ...'[5]

The Greeks reached home on February 1st, 1440 to be greeted by a hostile populace convinced that their traditional faith had been betrayed. Clerics and laity who had not been in Italy boycotted the unionists and their religious services. The Byzantine capital was split by the doctrinal quarrel more than ever before. Many of those who had signed the decree of union in Italy now in Constantinople repudiated their signatures. Patriarch Joseph II had died in Florence and been buried in the church of S. Maria Novella, where his tomb is still to be seen. In Constantinople a successor, Metrophanes, a unionist, was elected but received little help from the Emperor to implement the union, because in the beginning he was in isolated court-mourning for the death of his wife, the Empress Maria of Trebizond, and later probably because he was not desirous of forcing the convictions of others. Pope Eugenius, faithful to his promise, promoted a crusade, but the untimely death of Albert, King of the Romans, and the dynastic dispute that followed delayed its execution. In 1433 John Hunyadi had shown that Christian troops could beat the Turk. Unfortunately on November 10th, 1444 the crusade, led by Hunyadi and Ladislas, King of Hungary and Poland, was overwhelmed at Varna by a vastly superior force. Thereby one of the motives that might have recommended the union to the citizens of Constantinople was lost. Gregory Mammas, another unionist, followed Metrophanes as patriarch, but the tension did not abate. The anti-unionists had been skilfully led by Mark Eugenicus, Metropolitan of Ephesus, till his death in 1445. Scholarius, unionist in Italy, took up Mark's mantle in Constantinople and used his great abilities, cleverly and successfully, to render the decision of Florence of no effect. The unionist controversy dragged on for thirteen years, always growing more bitter. It was ended, and with it the union, when Mehmet II besieged and, on May 29th, 1453 captured the city, without any of the Latin States having sent troops to its defence. From the west only the Genoese mercenary Giustiniani and the papal legate, Cardinal Isidore, with the few troops in their pay and some ships from Venice, fought to save it. All but a handful of the Christian churches were in time turned into mosques, but the old schism between Greeks and Latins went on and is not healed even today.

The fall of Constantinople was the tragic close of a long and glorious history. Constantine the Great had founded a Christian

K

Empire, in which Church and State were but two aspects of one thing, with on the whole the imperial power dominating the ecclesiastical, while still being very sensitive to its influence. It had for centuries nursed and propagated the developing Christian faith. Facing the East, Byzantium had borne the brunt of the Arab and Turkish onslaughts and shielded the rest of Europe. Begun as the Latin-speaking Rome transplanted, it was soon assimilated into the Greek culture.

At every stage of its history there were men of learning, whether theologians or historians, students of medicine or of astronomy, who continued the ancient Greek tradition of letters. The language of Plato and Thucydides did not die. Their writings with those of many other authors of classical times were preserved in libraries, taught in schools, copied by scribes. By the time Constantinople fell, many of these manuscripts had been brought to the west and a host of exiled Greeks came with them, who made new copies that were scattered over all the countries of Europe. They testify to the culture and religion of the ancient Empire. But the most vivid witness today to the greatness of Byzantium is the Christian faith of its Orthodox descendants, which lives on after centuries of oppression to be still an inspiration to the world.

NOTES

1. Letter dated 12 July 1205 to Card. Legate of Syria who had hurried to Constantinople: P.L. 215, 701.

2. (a) Prof. of faith of Michael VIII Palaeologus, in *Acta Urbani IV, Clementis IV, Gregorii X (1261-1276)* (— Pont. Commissio ad redigendum Codicem Iuris Canonici orientalis, Fontes, Series III, vol. V. tom. I), ed. A. L. Tautu, Citta del Vaticano, 1953, pp. 120-1.

   (b) Letter of Metropolitans (ibid., p. 126).

3. Georgios Pachymeres, *De Michaele et Andronico Palaeologis*, vol. I, ed. I. Bekker, Bonn, 1835, lib. VI (pp. 456, 459).

4. Georgios Sphrantzes, *Memorii*, ed. V. Grecu. Bucharest, 1966 (p. 58).

5. *Quae supersunt Actorum Graecorum Concilii Florentini*, ed. J. Gill, Roma, 1953 (p. 462).

BIBLIOGRAPHY

For general reference *Cambrirdge Modern History*, vol. IV (2nd ed., 1966), chapters VII, VIII, IX, X, XII and XIX: Fliche, A. and Martin, V. (ed.). *Histoire de l'Eglise*, vol. 14 Le Grand Schisme, esp. Part IV, chapter 3, pp. 529–600, L'Union des Eglises.

Atiya, A. S., *The Crusade in the Later Middle Ages*. London, Methuen, 1938 and *The Crusade of Nicopolis*. London, Methuen, 1934.

Barker, J. W., *Manuel II Palaeologus 1391–1425. A Study in Late Byzantine Statesmanship*. Rutgers University Press, New Brunswick, 1969.

Dennis, G. T., *The Reign of Manuel II Palaeologus in Thessalonica*. Rome, 1960: Orientalia Christiana Analecta 159.

Gardner, A., *The Lascarids of Nicaea*. London, Methuen, 1912.

Geanakoplos, D. J., *The Emperor Michael Palaeologus and the West*. Harvard U.P., 1959 and *Greek Scholars in Venice*. Harvard U.P., 1962.

Gill, J., *The Council of Florence*, Cambridge U.P., 1959; and *Personalities of the Council of Florence*. Oxford, Blackwell, 1964.

Halecki, O., *Un Empereur de Byzance à Rome*. Warsaw, 1930.

Meyendorff, J., *A Study of Gregory Palamas*. London, 1964.

Miller, W., *The Latins in the Levant*. London, Murray, 1908; *Essays on the Latin Orient*. Cambridge U.P., 1921 and *Trezibond, the Last Greek Empire*. London, S.P.C.K., 1926.

Nicol, D. M., *The Despotate of Epirus*. Oxford, Blackwell, 1957.

Pears, E., *The Destruction of the Greek Empire*. London, Longmans, 1885.

Riggs, C. T. (trans.), *History of Mehmed the Conqueror by Kritovoulos*. Princeton U.P., 1954.

Runciman, S., *History of the Crusades*, vol. III. Cambridge U.P., 1954; *The Sicilian Vespers*. Cambridge U.P., 1958; and *The Fall of Constantinople*. Cambridge U.P., 1965.

Schlumberger, G., *Un Empereur de Byzance à Paris et à Londres*. Paris, 1916.

Setton, K., *Catalan Domination of Athens, 1311–1388.* Harvard U.P., 1948.

Smet, J., *Life of Saint Peter Thomas by Philippe de Mezières.* Rome, 1954: Textus et Studia Hist. Carmel II—for Graeco-Latin relations in XIVth century.

Wittek, P., *The Rise of the Ottoman Empire.* London, Royal Asiatic Society, 1938.

VII

Byzantine Art and Architecture
PHILIP WHITTING

Today there are many and magnificently illustrated books on Byzantine art guiding the careful student in the text and allowing him to reach his own conclusions from the plates. Fifty odd years ago there was very little on the subject in English. In 1911 O. M. Dalton published his *Byzantine Art and Archaeology*, a comprehensive work of reference well illustrated for its day and still very useful. But the beginner or the interested traveller had little to attract him, except Edith Browne's little book on architecture (1912). W. B. Yeats however, had visited Ravenna in 1907 and had been fascinated by the mosaics and culture of Byzantium, as was to appear in the 1920's in 'A Vision', 'Sailing to Byzantium' and 'Byzantium'. Between the wars David Talbot Rice began—originally and so fruitfully with Robert Byron—the work which he happily still continues, of interesting a much wider public in the claim that the Byzantines have contributed one of the great artistic traditions of the world. One ought also to mention the inspired comparison made by Clive Bell (*Art*, 1914) between the technique of the Byzantine mosaicist and that of the Post-Impressionists, particularly Signac and Seurat. A firm public had been established in France a little earlier by the work of Gabriel Millet and Ch. Diehl, who was a master of *vulgarisation* at its best. Diehl has said that the history of the Byzantine Empire was virtually recreated in the late nineteenth century, and interest in its art quickly followed. The overriding emphasis on the Renaissance, and through it on classical antiquity, had blotted out the intervening Middle Ages as something best avoided, even barbaric. The new interest both of scholars and of a widening public touched all European countries, including Russia which had a continuous Byzantine tradition. In 1940 the establishment of a centre of Byzantine Studies at Dumbarton Oaks has given renewed impetus to the interest both of scholars and of the general public in the United States, and indeed everywhere.

In recent years research over a wide field had been enormously expanded, while the ease and cheapening of travel has given large numbers of visitors to the Near East a chance to see and judge Byzantine art for themselves. These two strands have not exactly interwoven as developing scholarship has called in question previously accepted ideas and categories, leaving people—in any event somewhat unfamiliar with the names and history—in some confusion. In a short account such as this, which attempts to stress important lines of division and of development, some oversimplification must be forgiven. A whole new field of study has been opened since in 1926 Okunev discovered the original wall-paintings of the Church of St. Pantaleimon at Nerezi (near Skopje) under layers of plaster: the church had been built in 1164 and here was a firm dateline. Since that time a national effort has been made in Yugoslavia, Bulgaria and Romania to uncover, preserve and publish wall paintings. The material available is vast as one distinguishing characteristic of Byzantine church adornment was 'overall decoration', the covering of the entire wall and roof spaces. At Dečani in Yugoslavia there are alone above a thousand separate compositions: the figure highlights the different scale of patronage in East Europe and in the West. The wall paintings extend from the eleventh century to long after 1453 in the Balkans and offer a fine field for stylistic analysis, as do the more controversial schemes used in Anatolian churches. Particularly in these latter the scientific analysis of paint layers has brought a new aid to accuracy in dating, but even without this Kurt Weitzmann of Princeton in the field of manuscript illumination by careful consideration of style has achieved remarkable precision. In spite of all these advances the problems of Byzantine art history remain comparable with those in sociology, politics and economics.

1a (*above*)
Mosaic - *Crucifix*ion:
St. Luke in Stiris (Greece)

1b (*right*)
Mosaic - *Anastasis*: Nea
Mone (Chios)

2a (*left*)
Mosaic – *Crucifixion*:
Daphni (Greece)

2b (*below*)
Church of the Dormition
from the NE: Daphni
(Greece)

3a Mosaic – *Leo VI*: Holy Wisdom (Istanbul) narthex

3b Mosaic – *Deesis*: Holy Wisdom (Istanbul) gallery

4a (left)
Mosaic – *First Seven Steps of the Virgin*: Kariye Camii (Istanbul)

4b (below)
Wall Painting – *Anastasis*: Kariye Camii (Istanbul)

5a Enamels - *Crown of St. Andrew* (Buda Pest): Constantine IX - Zoe - Theodora

5b Ivory - *The Veroli Casket* (London)

6a (*left*) Mosaic – *Virgin Hodegetria*:
Kariye Camii (Istanbul)

6b (*right*) Ivory – *Constantine VII*
(Moscow)

7a Imperial Palace - *Tekfur Saray*: (Istanbul)

(i) (ii) (iii)

(iv) (v) (vi) (vii)

7b Coins (i) Alexius I : hyperper : rev (ii) John II : hyperper : rev (iii) Heraclius : solidus : obv & rev (iv) Justinian I : solidus : obv (v) Justinian II : solidus of 692 : obv (vi) Leo III & Constantine V : solidus : obv & rev (vii) Nicephorus II : solidus : rev.

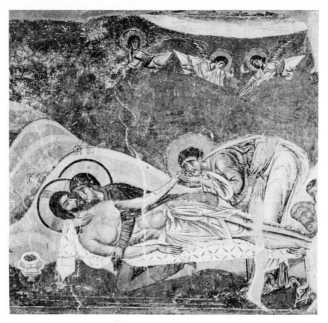

8a Wall Painting - *Lamentation* : Nerezi (Yugoslavia

8b Mosaic - *Pantocrator* : Fetiye Camii (Istanbul)

All through it has been clear that the period of Iconoclasm (726–843) was the crucial one in the artistic field, and recent work has only reinforced this. The iconoclast movement, complicated as it is, coincides with the arrival of the so-called 'Isaurian' dynasty (717–802) and is a convenient point for both historical and artistic division. Historically, military leaders with ideas associated with the Anatolian part of the Empire came to power. Artistically Iconoclasm represented the dominance of an aniconic artistic tradition which can be perhaps too easily associated with Anatolia. The dispute had been going on for a long time and the still existing decoration of the narthex in Justinian's Church of the Holy Wisdom is one simply of crosses. Whatever the origins, the world of art was as much disrupted as was that of religion. It is unfortunate that the part played by artists in Asia Minor, and the dating of the great cycles they produced at Göreme in particular, is still uncertain, but scholars are steadily shedding more light upon them and excellent reproductions photographic and otherwise are becoming available. There is no doubt, however, that Iconoclasm does provide the great watershed although the Emperor Theophilus was giving a new and impressive artistic stimulus just *before* it ended. Even the disaster of 1204 or political and economic eclipse of the empire in the fourteenth century could not prevent Byzantine art pursuing a course recognisably stemming from the reaction against Iconoclasm in the later ninth century. This reaction reaches a peak under the Comneni just before the Fourth Crusade then to thrive in centres away from the capital, only to return with the Emperors in 1261, with renewed vigour and brilliance. Political disasters did not go hand in hand with artistic decline. It is perhaps fairer to treat the whole post-iconoclastic period for the present as one long period, within which stages, greater or less in importance, may be identified. In all of these the key may be found in the classical past from which the Byzantines continually drew refreshment for their artistic ideas. Possibly the very difficulty of combining models from antiquity with the primary purpose of expressing the divine intelligibly in human terms, provided such a challenge as to produce artistic excellence. The problem is apparent in say the mosaic of Leo VI (886–912) in Constantinople over the entrance to the Church of the Holy Wisdom from its narthex—and is unsolved there—or in the vision of Ezekiel in the manuscript of St. Gregory made for Leo's father Basil I, and now in Paris.

It is time to look at the other, and earlier, side of the watershed. Here it is necessary to establish what kind of art pervaded the empire of Constantine the Great before he organised his capital at Constantinople and virtually changed the established religion of the Empire. The impact of both actions was important and from it developed the characteristic features of Byzantine art in its first apogee in the sixth century. It was the ambitions of Justinian I (527–565) and his extensive patronage of the arts especially in a building programme, secular and ecclesiastical, that gave wide prominence to the work of Byzantine artists, architects and engineers. The arts were media for spreading the Byzantine way of life and culture into a world where Roman security had been overwhelmed by Barbarian immigration. Presents from the Emperor of ivories, silks, icons, cloisonné enamelled objects and even of mosaics by sending the men who could make them, were treasured where such sophisticated products could neither be made, nor even contemplated. The most spectacular success story of this kind of official propaganda comes from the report of the envoys of Prince Vladimir of Kiev: what they saw in Constantinople 'passed human understanding' and the celebration of the liturgy in the church of the Holy Wisdom seemed to bring heaven to earth. Their story no doubt helped in persuading Prince Vladimir to adopt Orthodox Christianity as the religion of the Kievan state, thereby causing Russia to become a province of Byzantine art, architecture, law and much else, which outlasted the Byzantine Empire itself.

Thus were art and religion used for secular purposes, and for the Byzantines there was no real difference between the secular and the ecclesiastical. The Universal Church would one day

rule the world and sooner or later the Empire, which represented it on earth would achieve its objective in making the
earthly Empire a successful foreshadowing (mimesis) of the
heavenly one. Defeats and setbacks were only temporary and
due to a falling away of standards within the Empire itself. The
artist therefore had the task of conveying the overall objective
as well as the special one of representing the divine in terms
intelligible to human beings without undermining its majesty.
The literary descriptions of palaces show them to have been
very like monasteries in construction with their domes and
ancilliary buildings: they were decorated with mosaics too and
these, when avowedly secular, were full of allusions to the
Christian and imperial story with its foreshadowings in the Old
Testament and in classical antiquity. The whole world of art
was full of these allusions, such as Hercules' journey to the
realm of Pluto reminding the viewer of the Anastasis where
Jesus breaks the gates of Hell and raises Adam and Eve to the
glorious resurrection: both were symbolic of the conquest of
man's lower nature. One can understand why 'painters' guides'
were necessary to remind artists what should be contained in
any given picture and where it should go. Even if the theme
is the same and the particular scene the same, the remarkable
thing is how individual the approach of the artist could be.
That set types and patterns were endlessly copied in Byzantine
art is true, but that the results were flat and mechanical is not.

Within a culture and art which is clearly individualised and
called by us 'Byzantine' lay a tension implicit in the Empire's
history and geographical position. The pull of eastern and of
western ideas with first one dominant and then the other, was
to be found in all walks of life, and very clearly in the practice
of the arts. If eastern ideas tended to dominate the religious
sphere, the artist found continual refreshment from western
and Hellenistic springs. The idealistic naturalism of Graeco-
Roman art met an ascetic, harder realism from the east (from
Syria and Anatolia especially) and Constantinople with its
wealth of patronage was to prove a mixing ground for the re-

finement of both. In the sixth century and again in the twelfth something like a perfect balance was achieved in, for example, the mosaics of S. Apollinare Nuovo at Ravenna and the ivories, mosaics and gold coinage of the Comneni. When in the Iconoclastic period the East appeared to dominate both religion and art, the imbalance was plain to see and the reaction against it long-lasting. This is not to say that iconoclasm meant an end to art, as is sometimes assumed owing to the varied uses of the word. This is far from the case, but artists were driven into limited channels of expression as had been their lot in islamic lands. The great apsidal cross in the church of the Holy Peace in Constantinople—an early product of Iconoclasm—with its patterns and lettering around it, is something of great beauty, but lacking humanity. If single words be needed, the West stressed *humanity* and the East *asceticism*. Without humanity and the colour of nature art can become a matter of formal patterns.

In the fourth century the artistic impulses of the Roman Empire were Graeco-Roman or Hellenistic in so far as the widely spread official art went, though a different popular style flourished in Greece and Anatolia which was later to have important influence. When the capital was fixed at Constantinople it was in an area that had never wholly accepted the Roman official pattern of art, and this was where early Byzantine art was bred in the revolutionary circumstances of the religious change to Christianity. The ingredient of Hellenism, however, was never to be forgotten and even a thousand years later proved a powerful influence. It was a good fifty years before Christian art developed into a force to be reckoned with, not until the death of Theodosius I in 395 when paganism had been effectively defeated and its mysteries banned both in public and private. The catacombs of Rome, where much of the decoration is post-Constantinian, were painted by the leading artists of the day with a mixture of pagan, Old Testament and Christian scenes. The large number of Old Testament scenes arises from the Jews having been officially recognised earlier and having developed pictorial cycles of their own which could often be adopted by Christians as fortelling the new dispensation, like those of Jonah and Daniel. The same kind of meaning could be conveyed by the pagan stories of Alcestis, Hercules or Orpheus charming the animals with his lyre. Jesus in person or in allegory appears as the Sun lighting the world, the fisher, the hunter and the shepherd of souls: a sermon on the mount is preached to sheep on the hillside, there are orants, consecrated bread at ritual feasts and peacocks with their incorruptible flesh, the last a theme to have a long and entrancingly beautiful life in Byzantine art. The painters were working in a style and on subjects they were perfectly at home with. Christians as yet demanded nothing new and this early work in a Christian setting is sophisticated and competent, not primitive as is often imagined. Christian iconography could be adapted from existing designs: artists were accustomed to showing the Emperor receiving divine honours, such as were now to be given to Jesus.

Christians received lavish sums from Constantine and his successors for the construction of churches on a grand scale and official patronage brought a demand for art which had not been present in the primitive Church. The plans chosen were the well-tried *Basilica* which seemed capable of adaptation to any purpose, law court, gymnasium, market or synagogue, and the *Rotunda, Mausoleum* or *Martyrium*. Both were well known, the basilica capable of large expansion by adding multiple aisles, the martyrium centrally planned, more intimate, more individual, less easily extended and demanding a dome. In architecture as in painting the Christians took what they found and adapted it to their needs: a typical Christian addition to the basilica was the transept to show and light the altar to the east. Their literature shows no interest in the decorative arts and sculpture in the round was to be one of the casualties of the religious change. Sculpture seems to peter out in the fifth century with a large series of deeply drilled and technically masterly sarcophagi in which the merging of Hellenistic and

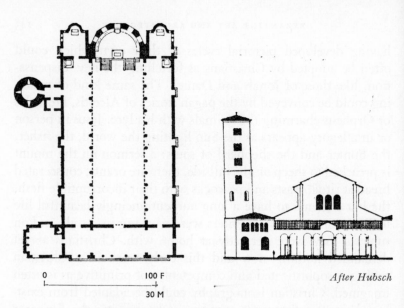

After Hubsch

S. APOLLINARE IN CLASSE, NEAR RAVENNA
(*Basilica plan*)

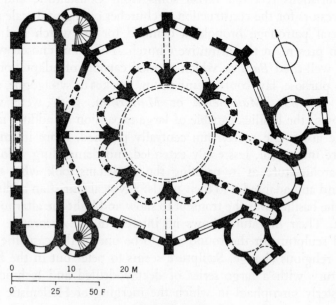

SAN VITALE, RAVENNA
(*Rotunda plan*)

more popular styles can be traced. Professor Pevsner has noted another casualty in the vast vaulting schemes undertaken under Diocletian, Maxentius and Constantine in Rome which come to a stop, until two hundred years later when Justinian's architects began to work on a comparable scale. As against such losses must be placed the development of glass mosaic wall pictures which were soon to become one of the most admired products of the Byzantine culture.

By the fifth century something like an integrated Christian art began to emerge and in the sixth century this blossomed into a period of great and many-sided artistic achievement. Until the reign of Justinian I there is all too little to go upon, but in glass mosaic particularly some fine work remains, especially in Italy and in Thessalonica. Although the Romans had brought the craft of laying marble floor mosaic to a fine art, it seems that they made little use of glass mosaic wall pictures. Both at Pompeii and Herculaneum there are, however, surviving examples showing technical skill in complicated designs and, after a long interval, some in the catacombs of Rome where the medium would be a useful one in reflecting any light that there was. Christians were to make much of this apparently neglected technique and a visit to the Mausoleum of Galla Placidia at Ravenna—she died in 450—shows its full glory in illuminating that small and, from the outside, apparently ill-lit space. The whole surface is enriched so that where marble revetment ceases, mosaic begins on the curving surfaces leading to the low dome. It was these curving surfaces that mosaic craftsmen were to delight in using, as can already be seen in the little apsidal mosaic of the chapel of the Holy David at Thessalonica and in the badly damaged but still strikingly effective decoration of the Baptistery of Soter (or S. Giovanni) at Naples, both perhaps a little earlier than Galla Placidia's mausoleum. It is worth comparing the apse at Holy David which shows the vision of Ezekiel around the youthful Jesus seated in the Universe, with the work in the Baptistery as two differing styles are to be seen which are to combine effectively a little later. At

Holy David the colour scheme of purple, green, grey and blue set off by glittering gold is low in tone and the figures only here and there show the linear beauty of Hellenistic art: but the overall effect is of awe and reverence. At Naples the vivid colouring and naturalistic portrayal of plants, animals and men make an immediate impression: this is a world in which the westerner is more at home. These two mosaics show the essential ingredients of Byzantine art—Hellenism with its strong linear approach, fluttering draperies and well-tried patterns, the naturalism and colour of the West, and the other-worldliness and subdued tones of the Eastern style. Another important monument of this period in Thessalonica is the round church of St. George with its mosaic of finely disposed architectural features and figures on a ground of gold. The churches of Rome provide a series of mosaics from those in Santa Constanza, the mausoleum of Constantine the Great's daughter, right up to Renaissance times, but their frequent restoration and the individual style of the craftsmen make them less useful as examples in a short account such as this.

The age of Justinian I provides at last ample material, literary and otherwise, from which the character of Byzantine art can be clearly judged. The arts reflect and are a part of the great ambitions of the Emperor to reassert the supremacy of the Roman Empire over the barbarians who had conquered so much of it in the west, and over the Persians whose King of Kings had for centuries asserted rival claims to Rome in the east. Justinian may have failed overall, but he had considerable success and perhaps greatest of all in his patronage of the arts. In his reign a break was made with the standard basilica/martyrium plans in architecture and a whole range of experiments was undertaken. The best known of these was the Church of the Holy Wisdom in Constantinople, which subtly combined the basilica and martyrium plans with remarkable technical skill, and still stands as one of the great architectural achievements of the world. For the Byzantines, however, it was a blind alley which the Turks were to explore after 1453 as a

mosque plan easily adaptable to any size. Byzantines in Justinian's reign had the confidence to undertake experiments such
as those at San Vitale in Ravenna and S. Sergius and Bacchus in
Constantinople, and had uncommon technical skill to reinforce
it such as was shown when Anthemius of Tralles and Isidore
of Miletus planned their flattened dome over one hundred feet
wide at the Holy Wisdom: contemporaries likened it to the
firmament of Heaven high above them.

All this building, including a comprehensive scheme of
frontier defence, was good propaganda for the renascent Empire and Procopius has left a major work, *On the Buildings*, in
this vein. The mosaic decoration of the churches was as impressive as their planning. Ravenna provides a whole range of sixth-
century schemes of which that at San Vitale with Justinian himself and Theodora in panels on either side of the altar, and S.
Apollinare Nuovo where an Ostrogothic design was finished
by Justinian, may be singled out. In San Vitale, Justinian and his
court stand full faced in the forward-looking pose which is
already a characteristic feature in manuscript illumination as
in mosaic. In S. Apollinare Nuovo restoration has flattened and
dimmed the glitter of the original mosaic setting but the com-
pelling vigour of its schemes of virgins and martyrs proceeding
up the nave to the altar puts one in mind of Macbeth's 'will
the line stretch out to th' crack of doom?' The repetitive linear
emphasis with the tall figures divided by palms in a landscape
of gold is typical of much Byzantine art.

The technique used by the Byzantines in setting mosaics was
a complicated one involving a first layer of plaster quickly
covered by a second, or setting bed, often pink in colour from
powdered brick, on which the outlines of the design and
placing of any inscriptions were sketched: into this last bed
the shanks of the mosaic tesserae were pressed. By having two
layers of plaster the moisture retained in the earlier one could be
brought up by finger pressure to soften the later one and so
allow tesserae to be inserted more easily. The standing Virgin
in the nave of the Kariye Camii clearly shows the sketch under-

L

neath and where a large mosaic needed to be done in sections, the junction lines can be seen at close quarters.

As the pictures were generally high above the viewer, the tesserae were angled down, the angle varying according to the height, and were set so as to project from the plaster, allowing light to come through the glass of which they were mainly composed: if gold or silver leaf was used in the tesserae, projection from the plaster was unnecessary as light could not come through it. Viewed at close quarters the surface of the mosaic is rough with much plaster visible between the lines of tesserae, but their angling prevents any of this being seen from below. When portraying important features such as the human face the tesserae are placed close together and the colours used, however impressionistic they may appear, give from below a natural effect. A wide range of colours was available and the mosaicist's 'palette' for the Leo VI picture in the Church of the Holy Wisdom, included fifty-two different shades. Much has been discovered about mosaic technique in the course of recent restoration work in Constantinople, and students in the Academy of Fine Arts in Ravenna have copied some of the sixth-century pictures there, employing the old techniques in making and using the tesserae. In the late nineteenth century, restorers tended to flatten the surface, as was the current practice in mosaic making, and reset the tesserae entirely, within the limits of the old design. In one case—a bust of Justinian I in Ravenna—it can be shown from photographs that not a single tessera remains in its original position.

Byzantine mosaic decoration was closely associated with the architectural forms it adorned. Domes raised on squinches or pendentives, semidomes and apses and vaulting itself provided precisely the curving spaces that concentrated light and brought out the best in mosaic craftsmen. In the VIth century especially, Byzantine buildings had little to recommend them on the outside: one aim was to keep the sun out so that windows were few and tended to be high up. Mosaic was a fine medium to make the most of what light there was inside and corresponded in function to the stained glass windows of colder northern climes where it was necessary to make full use of the sun. Decoration was concentrated and spread all over the interior with free use of stucco and symmetrically cut (opus Alexandrinum) marble revetments in contrast to the exterior showing thin bricks in heavy layers of mortar—the normal materials used. There was almost more mortar than brick and until patterns were made of the bricks, with striking effect in the thirteenth and fourteenth centuries, as in the Church of the Holy Apostles in Thessalonica, Byzantine exteriors were only notable for the pattern of construction and above all for the beauty of their domes.

The reign of Justinian has led to elaboration on the themes of mosaic and architecture but it cannot be left before saying something of silk and ivory. By methods akin to modern industrial espionage, silkworms were brought to Constantinople and reared successfully: as a result imperial workshops—a mono-poly—were set up which in succeeding centuries were to pro-duce some of the finest fabrics of their day, highly prized by the kings and princes who received them. Today fragments, retrieved from the tombs of saints and rulers, give some idea of their richness of colour and of their designs which were often of Persian character with panels of animals or scenes facing one another. Perhaps the finest is the shroud of St. Germain at Auxerre and the Victoria and Albert Museum has excellent examples. Ivory carving had been one of the crafts carried over from the Roman Empire and it continued to be practised especi-ally in the form of consular diptychs—official presents in the form of two folding ivory leaves. Several diptychs for Justinian himself as consul survive: but especially in the east more elabo-rate work was being undertaken. After iconoclasm ivory carvers produced work of the highest quality, much copied in southern Europe, which became a luxury product typical of Byzantine workmanship at its best.

Already in Justinian's reign money for patronage was run-ning out in the face of increasing pressure from enemies on the northern frontiers and from the Sassanian dynasty in Persia. His successors were on the defensive and even the capital itself was under attack. In Heraclius' reign the Empire was virtually extinguished but for its capital, its navy and its army: but in 629 the Sassanians were at last, and absolutely defeated. Respite was not to come, as the Arabs were beginning the attacks which swept away the south-eastern provinces of the Empire for ever and overwhelmed what was left of Persia as well. This was the seed-bed from which the régime of the 'Isaurian' dynasty and the policy of Iconoclasm grew: it was a crisis demanding a fundamental rethinking of ends and means.

The Iconoclast Emperors had to put their major emphasis on military survival and reconquest, but this was backed by an ideology which brought eastern ideas flooding back into religion and art. It was considered that Christian pictures were given too much adoration in themselves rather than for the ideas and persons that they represented, and therefore they must be removed. Round the apse of the Church of the Holy Wisdom in Constantinople which now contains a mosaic of the Virgin and Child is a mosaic inscription which can with certainty be restored as reading 'The images which the impostors had formerly cast down, here the pious Emperors have again set up'. The condition of the gold background of the apse seems to indicate the elimination of a large cross, such as can still be seen near by in the Church of the Holy Peace, before its replacement by the 'Virgin and Child' which would rightfully be expected in the apse. The picture now visible may be largely a fourteenth-century restoration, but the inscription with the iconoclasts as 'impostors' and Theodora and her son Michael III as the 'pious Emperors' seems to apply well to the process described above. The gold coinage shows another aspect of what was happening: here the bust of Jesus recently introduced as the normal obverse design and the long-standing reverse design of a cross on steps were both removed. In their place Leo III and his son Constantine V occupy obverse and reverse respectively. The images of the Emperors, which also received divine honours, were not under ban and right through the iconoclastic period only the imperial family appears on the gold coinage.

There must have been much destruction of mosaics and of icons, and recent research has shown it to have extended far beyond the capital and its environs. Both in the now destroyed Church of the Dormition at Nicaea and in the Holy Wisdom at Thessalonica pictures of the Virgin in the apses replaced crosses once put there by the iconoclasts. The choir of the latter church contains a mosaic vault with an abstract pattern of the iconoclastic period: but more representative of what was artistically possible under iconoclasm are the lush pictures of riverine landscapes and unrealistic Hellenistic buildings uncovered between the Wars in the courtyard of the Great Mosque at Damascus, put up by Byzantine craftsmen about 715. Decorative schemes had to be abstract or aniconic and this applied to the humble churches of the Peloponnese or Cappadocia, as in the Emperor Theophilus' additions to the imperial palace. The same kind of ban operated in islamic countries and allowed for pictures and patterns of great beauty: but so far as Byzantine artists were concerned only the subjects had to be different, and they could exploit the animal kingdom denied to Moslem artists.

Iconoclasm represented strong currents of opinion in the Empire but the persecution and restrictions which had for so long accompanied the régime caused a reaction clear in its implications, widespread even in Asia Minor, and to last a long time. It should be added that in western Europe and in the Abbasid empire there was also a contemporary artistic revival. Yet it is well to recall that the impressionistic style of portraiture developed by die engravers for the busts of Emperors on coins, was to last for over a century more. This medium is traditionally a conservative one, but in fact on coins the two styles carried on alongside one another, and almost immediately a naturalistic bust of Jesus, copied from coins of 692, was restored to the obverse of gold solidi. Artists had been able to learn much in the period however, and were to turn it to good use.

The Macedonian dynasty (886–1056) was to inspire an unprecedented loyalty in the inhabitants of the capital at least: it was to provide emperors resourceful in action, contemplative, literary, artistic and dedicated to the arts of war—though naturally not all at once. The period was one of wealth and confidence though disasters were looming towards its end. Artistic periods do not always neatly coincide with dynastic or political ones, as was broadly the case under the Iconoclasts. Figure painting, religious and secular, had returned to stay and a series of 'classical' revivals took place in which styles, detail and stories from antiquity were rediscovered and blended with current practice. A continuous and subtle change was in progress, of which one, taking place around 1050, has recently been charted by Kurt Weitzmann from illuminated manuscripts which are capable of fairly exact dating. Equally with little in the way of dates to go upon, the progress of change in mosaic decoration can be seen from the Holy Luke in Stiris of early XIth century, through that of Nea Mone in Chios and the Holy Wisdom in Kiev, to that in the Church of the Dormition at Daphni where the latest of the craftsmen were working around 1100. If the picture of Leo VI in the Holy Wisdom be compared with the Pantocrator in the dome at Daphni—regarded as one of the greatest of Byzantine creations—or with the Crucifixion in the same church, the change in the two centuries between them is clear enough, but the leaven at work is the same. Take two elements in the Leo VIth picture, the roundel of St. Michael (or is he Mercury?) and the figure of the prostrated Emperor himself: the former only integrated into the design, if it can be called so at all, by a balancing roundel, is as Hellenistic as it could be: but Leo VI, alike in his posture and the unnaturalistic curves and triangles with which it is portrayed, is a splendid example of what could be done by impressionist techniques. In the Daphni pictures integration has been successfully achieved.

The mosaic cycles at Holy Luke, Nea Mone and Daphni, magnificent in themselves, were displayed in the new architectural setting of the cross-in-square planned church which is characteristic of the post-iconoclastic centuries, and has been called 'the most perfect of all Byzantine plans'. Churches were generally smaller in the west but capable of much variation. Basically as at Daphni the cross is outlined within the square by higher walls and vaults and at the crossing was placed a dome raised on a drum. The eleventh-century domes at Holy Luke and Daphni may be quoted as outstanding examples. In this style there was more light inside and more decoration, of windows and string courses especially, outside. The plan can be split into several sub-varieties of which one with domes on the corners of the square as well as at the crossing, is often met.

In the schematic synopsis appended to this chapter to help the understanding of this short account of a long and complicated period, the date 1025 has been arbitrarily selected as the end of the first stage of the classical revival. No exact date can yet be established, or indeed is likely to be, but a division at least emphasises that change is continuing. One object—the ivory 'Veroli' casket now in the Victoria and Albert Museum—will serve to underline how classical in character the art of the time could be. If taken together these caskets form a large class of objects and have been dated to the fifth, sixth and later centuries: the Veroli casket, a piece of eminent technical skill and great beauty is now attributed to around the year 1000. Many Graeco-Roman details could be urged to justify a much earlier dating and only by stages have doubts been removed: one panel shows Europa personified with a shawl above her head (as much tenth-century manuscript illumination shows) riding jauntily on her bull towards a vicious-looking crowd grouped as for the stoning of Achan. Ivory carving reached remarkable heights in the tenth to twelfth centuries, whether in single panels or diptychs which were really icons, book covers or more elaborate pieces with many panels. A number of panels represent the 'Virgin who Shews the Way' (that is, standing with Jesus on her left arm), and the Victoria and Albert Museum—a collection rich in ivories—has a unique example of this subject sculptured in the round and of the same period. Other ivories show members of the Macedonian dynasty like Leo VI (Berlin) Constantine VII (Dumbarton Oaks and a superb piece in Moscow Museum of Fine Arts) and Romanus II (Paris).

Cloisonné enamel plaques were another luxurious product of these centuries. The technique had been practised in Byzantine lands in the VIth century or before but it was not until the Xth and subsequent centuries that it was done on a considerable scale and began to take a major place among the arts: the products were much sought after in the West. These objects were indeed luxurious as gold was the best metal in which to work, beginning with a gold back-plate and soldering onto it gold wire bent into the shapes required by the design: the minute partitions (cloisons) thus formed were then filled with glass coloured by metal oxides and finally polished level. The work required technical skill of a high order and immediately gained the prestige and exercised the charm that it has since retained. It was a suitable imperial gift and Constantine IX made one such to King Andrew I of Hungary, a crown of cloisonné panels which may still be seen in Budapest: three of the panels contain representations of the Emperor, his wife Zoe and her sister Theodora, the two ladies being the last members of the Macedonian dynasty to rule. Considering the skill required and the great value of these plaques, mention must be made of the *Pala d'Oro* altarpiece in St. Marks, Venice where eighty-six plaques have been brought together in a masterpiece of the jeweller's art. Some of these were ordered from Byzantine craftsmen in the Xth century but many additions (some of them of Venetian manufacture) were made in subsequent centuries and are of uneven quality. Some chalices in the Treasury of St. Marks, brought back from Constantinople by the Fourth Crusaders are embellished with cloisonné enamel settings and are as fine examples of Byzantine craftsmanship and beauty as can be found. Jewellers would probably also be die engravers for the coinage and under the Comnene dynasty a remarkably high standard of design and technical execution was achieved on the gold hyperpers. There had been an increasing debasement of the metal used from around 1040 until the end of the century when Alexius I restored the fineness to 21½ carats, something near to its old standard. Some of his own hyperpers show an interesting example of perspective in which the observer seems to be in front and below the magnificent figure of the Emperor whose head, touched by the Hand of God, is very small compared with the exaggerated length of his body: his left hand is thrust forward showing the jewelled decoration, strikingly large, on the inside of his cloak, while his right hand is held back with the same decoration of the cloak appearing very much smaller. Another coin shows Alexius' son John II standing beside the Virgin: much more naturalistic and less dramatic than the other, there is the same strong linear effect, heightened in both cases by the legend being disposed in vertical blocks instead of in the more usual circular form. Artists of quality were at work and they achieved beauty in articles of daily use.

It was while the Comnene dynasty occupied the throne that artists took a perceptible turn towards a more natural portrayal of the human body and of human emotions. The hieratic attitudes masking emotion with a divinely supported peace of mind, had been a standard form only occasionally discarded. The future was to lie with the more naturalistic approach of the artist in the John II coin as against the remoteness and impressionist technique achieved in the coin of Alexius I. In scenes such as the 'Deposition from the Cross', the human body becomes a thing of weight, not a mystical symbolic image bridging the human and divine, and the bystanders with dramatic movements give full rein to their distraught emotions. The trend may be characterised as humanism and by the end of the twelfth century it seems firmly implanted in artistic circles. It is a part of the classical revival and one particularly appealing to western eyes. What is noteworthy is that it had gathered sufficient strength to survive the Latin interlude that followed the Fourth Crusade. Many artists seem to have left the capital and continued their creative work in Balkan centres, helping and inspiring the national schools developing in Serbia and Bulgaria. This humanism is to be seen clearly informing the artists employed on the wall-paintings at Nerezi soon after the Church of St. Panteleimon was built in 1164. They were almost certainly from the capital but their lead was soon to be taken up widely in the Balkans so that the Latin interlude of 1204–1261 was not artistically disastrous: a visit to the Yugo-slav churches at Studenica, Mileševa and Sopoćani or to the Holy Wisdom at Trebizond conclusively refutes any such thought. The style was mature and ready for new development. This continuity makes for difficulty in the dating of some out-standing pictures. One such is the Deesis mosaic in the gallery of the Holy Wisdom at Constantinople, a badly damaged pic-ture fortunately still retaining most of its upper part, including heads of the Virgin, Jesus and John the Baptist. It has been dated to the early and to the late twelfth century and after the Latin period by highly competent authorities. It seems to breathe humanism and for that reason the choice should per-haps be made between the two last alternatives; but the problem itself underlines the difficulty of making hard and fast cate-gories in the post-iconoclastic period. Owing to the wealth of material in the form of wall-paintings now becoming available in Greece, Yugoslavia, Bulgaria, Cyprus and other places these problems seem likely to be resolved in time, just as recent dis-coveries at St. Catherine's Monastery at Mt. Sinai have helped in dating icons. What is clear is that a vigorous phase of artistic achievement was in progress at a time when the Empire both politically and economically was in dire straits.

It can be seen that the 'Palaeologan Renaissance', once re-garded as a post-1261 phenomenon, must be considered in relation to the period of the Comneni and not in isolation. Some work done in the early fourteenth century can challenge the best ever produced in the millennium of the Byzantine Empire, particularly the mosaics of the Kariye Camii (Holy

Saviour in Chora) and Fetiye Camii (Panagia Pammakaristos) in Constantinople. In both may be observed a faithful
adherence to nature and a return to Hellenistic forms especially
in the architectural details and above all a gentle humanism
which may have themselves been copied from tenth-century
illuminations. The recent restoration of both churches with
scholarly care by the Byzantine Institute in Istanbul has been a
work of major importance in that the visitor, to the Kariye
Camii in particular, has a real opportunity to take himself back
into the brilliant colours and glitter of marble and mosaic
characteristic of Byzantine churches, besides being able to study
in detail the picture cycles of the life of the Virgin and of the
infancy and ministry of Jesus. In the mortuary chapel built
alongside is a fresco of the Anastasis which must be amongst
the finest produced in the Palaeologan period. Both in mosaic
and wall-painting the style is the same with figures moving
with lively freedom in a blaze of colour, cleverly disposed
against a background full of picturesque natural detail and
queer architectural shapes culled from Hellenistic prototypes.
The tall, monumental and hieratic figures, impressive but im-
passive, have disappeared.

The pictorial schemes in the Kariye Camii remain in so complete a form and are so well preserved that their effect and
reputation is enhanced. The characteristics of the style can
really be seen at their best much earlier at Sopoćani in the
1260's. In mid-fourteenth century after the Kariye cycles
were produced, a new and academic twist, associated with the
work of Theophanes the Greek is given to Byzantine painting
introducing its last phase before the Turkish conquest.

In the thirteenth-century town of Mistra, which became
almost a second capital because it was out of the way of the
main line of Turkish expansion, there are many churches with
decorative schemes surviving to show the character of wall-
painting in the Palaeologan period. The Platonist scholar
Gemistos Plethon was a prominent member of the court: but
for humanism being so characteristic of artistic achievement

at the time, it might be thought that his influence had been
responsible for the work in the Peribleptos church and, particularly impressive, in the Pantanassa (1428), one of the last decorative schemes to be undertaken in the town. The style is
metropolitan in character and the 'Transfiguration' in the Peribleptos shows all that gentleness and felicity of colour which
makes the period so attractive. In the Pantanassa there is a
realism more usually associated with schools of artists at work
in the southern Balkans but the same sense of colour is there:
the 'Raising of Lazarus' and the 'Entry into Jerusalem' are
justly acclaimed as amongst the greatest achievements of the
period.[1]

The early fourteenth century saw another development of
mosaic art in the miniature, portative, mosaic icons. There
had been fine examples of this luxurious product made in
the twelfth century but most of this small and now widely
scattered group of objects appears to come from the Palaeologan
period, like the Victoria and Albert Museum's 'Annunciation'
(6″ × 4″) or the St. Theodore 'Stratilates' (6½″ × 2½″) at
Leningrad in which the floor pattern is the same. Only persons
of great wealth could afford such an icon and taken with new
church foundations being increasingly made by great nobles
rather than the Emperors, it may indicate the concentration of
wealth in the hands of a few nobles and high officials—men
like Theodore Metochites, the learned Grand Logothete, who
refounded the monastery of the Chora in Constantinople and
is still to be seen there, in his striped turban and figured gown
of green and gold, in mosaic.

Churches continued to be built and patterns in bricks were
ingeniously elaborated to adorn the exteriors, alternating
courses of brick and stone and the use of glazed tiles combining
to give a polychrome effect. They tended to be higher, often
with elaborate galleries, and domes were raised on taller drums.
In Yugoslavia near the battlefield of Kossovo the church of
Gračanica has corner domes rising to a height eight times their
width, though its brickwork is more restrained than that

found in Thessalonica's fourteenth-century churches. In Constantinople there was more experiment with plans than elsewhere. Separate chapels, or parecclesia, for commemorative family purposes were sometimes added as in the Church of the Chora, and that of Panagia Pammakaristos. In Epirus at Arta long basilicas continued to be built, with narrow aisles but with most ingenious polychrome patterns, and, also there, the externally clumsy Paragoritissa of cross-in-square plan is enlivened by its belvedere and the strange association of its trefoil gothic ornament and mosaics within. Unpopular as the Latin crusaders were in Byzantine lands they left much behind them, not least in architecture. The blending may well be seen in the Pantanassa (1428) at Mistra with its bell tower, open colonnade and fleur-de-lys ornament: it would hardly be out of place in the Tuscan hills. The Tekfur Saray—the remnant of the imperial palace near the land-walls of Constantinople—has the polychrome external decoration and balconies that mark fourteenth- and fifteenth-century construction, but its plan is western and work may have begun during the Latin occupation. Too little notice has been given in these pages to secular buildings but few remain intelligibly to the eye: the Tekfur Saray is an exception as are the magnificent fifth-century land-walls with their interesting repairs and additions.

The size of the shrinking Empire and the melancholy expectations of disaster voiced by its inhabitants seem to have had little effect on the enthusiasm of the artists in this extraordinarily lively Palaeologan period. They had still to interpret unity of the world of God, his saints and his followers: whatever the hard facts of the present due, no doubt, to their failings; men still knew that one day the Universal would reign supreme. But well before 1453 a certain academism is stiffening figures and overcrowding them with ground detail: designs seem less spontaneous. A new perhaps clinging desperately to the old instead of a found and overdue renaissance. Refugees before and after um' as a sympathetic reception in Venice—a 'second

Cardinal Bessarion called it—and in Crete, and large decorative schemes and church building could still be undertaken under the Turks, as Mount Athos and Romania can still bear witness: but cohesion was missing. A living art went on in Russia but, more broadly, it becomes a matter henceforth of tracing Byzantine artistic *influence*. Particular attention has been paid to Domenicos Theotocopoulos, the Cretan pupil of great Venetian masters who made his home in Spain, where he was called El Greco: the iconography of his 'Burial of Count Orgaz' brings to mind a Byzantine 'Dormition of the Virgin' and his tall, other-worldly figures and unusual colour schemes confirm the impression. More important is the similarity of the early fourteenth-century work done by Cimabue and Giotto with that done over a century before under the Comneni, and then the different turns taken by each. Modern artists have taken up again the Byzantine love of exploiting the texture of materials, and their interest in the abstract and impressionism. Perhaps this may account for some of the growing interest in the Byzantine Empire which might easily have succumbed altogether to the thunder of Gibbon's periods in his *Decline and Fall of the Roman Empire*. If a stand be taken in 1453 one sees an art founded in Hellenism finding its way back again after an experimental and refining period of over a millenium: in the course of it, a style of lasting significance was born. A few words from W. B. Yeats' 'A Vision' may help to explain: 'I think', he writes, 'that in early Byzantium, maybe never before or since in recorded history, religious, aesthetic and practical life were one . . .

NOTE

No mention has been made of the so-called 'Cretan and Macedonian' in the Palaeologan period. The names, geographically most misp are now fortunately being abandoned: broadly 'Cretan' stood for hi with a miniaturist quality, impressionist and with heavy white dr, 'Macedonian' for work with a more naturalistic, realistic and a 'pproach. That there were two styles—a Southern Balkan and shous evident, and analysis of the increasing material available e more satisfactory categories to be established.

BIBLIOGRAPHY

Ainalov, D. V., *Hellenistic Origins of Byzantine Art* (edn., Sobolevitch and Mango). Rutgers U.P., 1961 (p. 332 illustrated).

B.B.C., *Byzantium*. British Broadcasting Corporation, 1968 (p. 52, including 51 illustrations, some in colour). Designed to accompany a basic course on radio.

Beckwith, J., *The Art of Constantinople*. Phaidon Press, 1961 (p. 184, and well illustrated).

Dalton, O. M., *Byzantine Art and Archaeology*. Oxford, 1911 (p. 728, and well illustrated). Comprehensive and still indispensable for reference.

Diez, E. and Demus, O., *Byzantine Mosaics in Greece*. Harvard, 1931 (p. 124, and 151 illustrations): for Hosios Loukas, Nea Mone, and Daphni.

Grabar, A., *L'Iconoclasme Byzantin—Dossier Archéologique*. Paris, 1957 (p. 278, and 163 illustrations).

Grabar, A., *The Beginnings of Christian Art*, 1967 (p. 326); *Byzantium from the death of Theodosius to the Rise of Islam*, 1966 (p. 440). Both superbly illustrated, in Thames and Hudson's 'Arts of Mankind' series.

Kähler, H. and Mango, C., *Hagia Sophia*. Zwemmer, 1967 (p. 76, and 103 illustrations making a valuable photographic record of the Church of the Holy Wisdom).

Krautheimer, R., *Early Christian and Byzantine Architecture*. Penguin Books, 1965 (p. 367, and 192 plates). A fine, comprehensive work for reference.

Lazarev, V., *Old Russian Murals and Mosaics*. Phaidon, n.d.

Pierce, H. and Tyler, R., *L'Art Byzantin*. Paris 1932 and 1934. The second volume of 208 plates and descriptions is particularly good for Justinian I.

Radojčic, S., *Yugoslavia—Mediaeval Frescoes*. UNESCO, no date (p. 36, with 32 coloured plates).

Restle, Marcell, *Byzantine Wall Painting in Asia Minor*. Verlag Aurel Bongers, Recklinghausen, 1967, (3 vols. magnificently illustrated).

Talbot Rice, D., *The Art of Byzantium*. Thames and Hudson, 1959 (p. 348, including 240 illustrations with excellent descriptions).

Talbot Rice, D., *Byzantine Painting—The Last Phase*. Weidenfeld and Nicolson, 1968 (p. 224, and 199 illustrations).

Underwood, P. A., *The Kariye Djami*. Routledge and Kegan Paul, 1967, 3 vols., of which II and III are illustrations.

Vermeule, C. C., *Roman Imperial Art in Greece and Asia Minor*. Harvard, 1968 (p. 550, illustrated).

Weitzmann, K., Chatzidakis and others, *Icons from South Eastern Europe and Sinai*. Thames and Hudson, 1968 (p. 107, and 220 illustrations).

Weitzmann, K., *Greek Mythology in Byzantine Art*, Princeton, 1951.

	Dates	Period	Description
I.	330–395	Roman–Hellenistic	Rome centred—carrying on existing imperial and private art. Mixture of pagan, Old and New Testament themes as in catacombs of Rome. Spate of building.
II.	395–527	Integration	Byzantium as centre brings in more eastern influences especially of a less sophisticated type—these associated with Christianity. An integrated Hellenic/Christian art develops especially in mosaic.
III.	527–565	Justinian I	A period of imperial ambitions and artistic patronage. Architectural experiment—Church of the Holy Wisdom etc. A great age of many-sided activity, and confidence.
IV.	565–726	Decline	Too much had been attempted—defence of frontiers a primary consideration; internal insecurity. Social and religious tensions. Arabs sweep over S.E. provinces and Slavs over the Balkans.
V.	726–843	Iconoclasm	A great watershed in art—state control: military survival and reconquest the priority. Removal and destruction of religious pictures but new art forms devised: aniconic and impressionistic art. More eastern influence. New impetus given to arts under Theophilus.
VI.	843–1025	Classical Revival (a) Macedonians	Artists respond to a less restrictive atmosphere but iconoclastic styles survive: confidence returns: robust enthusiastic return to classical models. The cross-in-square church plan.
VII.	1025–1180	Classical Revival (b) Comneni	An integration of naturalism and monumental linear emphasis brings a peak of achievement. Humanity stressed as against formalism. Nerezi wall paintings 1164. Mosaics, ivories and enamels.
VIII.	1180–1330	Classical Revival (c) Palaeologi	Internal collapse and 4th Crusade lead to Latin Empire 1204–1261: but classical revival goes on in the Balkans—naturalism, intimacy, personal passion, gentle humanism and Hellenistic detail—and returns to Constantinople with the Palaeologan dynasty. Kariye Camii and Fetiye Camii represent the end of this period. Brick patterns and ceramic decoration in architecture.
IX.	1330–1453	Formalism sets in	Continued development of wall painting schemes in the Balkans and Greece, but gradually the impetus of the Classical Revival is exhausted. Increased copying, academism and hardening of lines and highlights. Theophanes the Greek in Russia.
X.	Post Byzantine		After 1453 Crete becomes the centre of a Byzantine style until conquest by the Turks 1669.

M

Chronology

A.D. 79   Destruction of Pompeii and Herculaneum.

224–630   Sassanian dynasty in Persia.

293   Diocletian's plan of two Emperors, each with a Caesar-successor.

305   Abdication of the Emperors Diocletian and Maximian.

306   Death of the Emperor Constantius, father of Constantine the Great.

312   Constantine's 'vision'—Victory at Milvian Bridge.

324   Constantine, victorious over Licinius, reunites the Roman Empire.

325   First Œcumenical Council at Nicaea to define the Christian faith, in view of Arianism.

330   Inauguration of the rebuilt Byzantium, now called Constantinople, as capital of the Empire.

337   Baptism and death of Constantine.

361–363   Pagan reaction under Julian 'the Apostate', the last of Constantine's dynasty.

364   Death of Jovian—Empire divided between Valentinian I (West) and his brother Valens (East).

378   Valens defeated and killed by the Goths at Adrianople.

379–395   Theodosius I—dynasty reigning until 457.

381   Second Œcumenical Council at Constantinople reaffirms anti-Arianism of Nicaea: Constantinople to take precedence next after Rome.

392   Pagan worship in public and private forbidden.

395   Empire divided between Arcadius (East) and Honorius (West).

408–450	Theodosius II—the walls of Constantinople built.
429–534	Vandal Kingdom in N. Africa.
431	Third Œcumenical Council at Ephesus—condemnation of Nestorius (stressing humanity of Jesus).
450	Death of Galla Placidia, daughter of Theodosius I: mausoleum at Ravenna.
451	Attila the Hun defeated at Chalons: death 453. Fourth Œcumenical Council at Chalcedon—condemnation of Monophysitism (stressing divinity of Jesus).
476	End of Roman Empire in the West: Odovacer rules from Ravenna, nominally under Emperor Zeno.
493–526	Reign of Theodoric the Great—founder of Ostrogothic kingdom of Italy.
507–711	Visigothic kingdom in Spain.
519	S. Apollinare Nuovo begun in Ravenna—later work 558.
527–565	Reign of Justinian I. His Empress Theodora died 548.
529	Codex Justinianus published; supplemented in 533 by the Pandects or Digest. University of Athens closed.
531–579	Khusru I ruler of Persia.
532	'Nika' riots in Constantinople: Church of the Holy Wisdom destroyed. 'Everlasting' peace with Persia.
532–547	Construction of San Vitale, Ravenna.
533–534	Belisarius reconquers N. Africa from Vandals.
535–540	Belisarius reconquers Sicily and Italy from Ostrogoths.
537	Dedication of new Church of the Holy Wisdom, Constantinople.
540	Belisarius recalled from Italy to oppose Persians who had captured Antioch. Ostrogothic revival under Totila.
542	Bubonic plague in Constantinople.
550	Avars (from Mongolia) reach Black Sea and establish control of nearby Slav tribes
550–551	Liberius reconquers part of southern Spain from Visigoths.

552	Narses defeats Totila at Busta Gallorum: end of Ostrogothic kingdom in 553.
553	Fifth Œcumenical Council at Constantinople—the Three Chapters denounced, as concession to Monophysites.
558	Justinian's treaty with Avars, giving them privileged status.
562	Treaty for 50 years with Persia.
565–578	Justin II.
568	Lombard invasion of Italy—Ravenna besieged 578.
574	Justin II buys off Avars and Slavs.
577	Invasions of Balkans by Avars and Slavs begin.
578–582	Tiberius II (adopted co-emperor by Justin II).
582–602	Maurice (adopted co-emperor by Tiberius II). Creation of Exarchates of Ravenna and Carthage.
591	Maurice supports Khusru II (590–628) in Persian civil war and makes advantageous treaty. Maurice attacks Avars but unable to get support for a long struggle.
602–610	Phocas Emperor after deposing and killing Maurice.
608	Revolt of Heraclius, father of the later Emperor, in Carthage. Persians overrun Asia Minor.
610–641	Reign of Heraclius after deposing and killing Phocas.
614	Persians capture Jerusalem and in 619 conquer Egypt.
622	Heraclius sets out on campaign against Persia. The Hijra—flight of the Prophet Muhammad to Medina.
626	Persians and Avars besiege Constantinople.
627	Heraclius defeats Persians at Nineveh: Holy Cross returned to Jerusalem in 629.
636–638	Arabs occupy Palestine (Jerusalem 638) and Syria.
640–646	Arabs occupy Egypt and overrun Persian Empire.
641–668	Reign of Constans II, grandson of Heraclius.
647	First Arab invasion of Asia Minor.
655	Byzantines defeated in first naval battle with Arabs.
674–678	First siege of Constantinople by Arabs.
c.680	Creation of the Bulgarian state.

680	Sixth Œcumenical Council condemns Monothelitism (Heraclius' compromise solution of the Nestorian/Monophysite problem).
711	Arab conquest of N. Africa completed—Carthage taken 698. End of the dynasty of Heraclius, with Justinian II.
715	Great Mosque at Damascus decorated with mosaic for Caliph Walid I.
717–741	Reign of Leo III of Syria, founder of the 'Isaurian' dynasty.
717–718	Second siege of Constantinople by the Arabs.
726–843	Period of Iconoclasm (interrupted 780–813).
730	Leo III's iconoclastic decrees.
740	Arabs defeated by Leo III at Acroinion.
741–775	Reign of Constantine V—victories over the Arabs.
750	Fall of Umayyad dynasty of caliphs—seat of caliphate moved from Damascus to Baghdad: the Abbasid dynasty.
751	Lombards capture Ravenna—end of Byzantine rule in N. and Central Italy.
754	Iconoclastic Council at Hieria.
756–775	War between Byzantium and Bulgaria.
783	Reconquest of Greece from Slavs begins.
787	Seventh Œcumenical Council—restoration of icon-worship.
800	Coronation of Charlemagne.
811	Nicephorus I defeated and killed by Bulgarians (Krum).
813–820	Leo V—iconoclasts return to power.
820–867	The Amorian dynasty (Michael III 842–867).
826	Death of Theodore the Studite.
838	Arab invasion of Asia Minor—fall of Amorium.
829–842	Reign of Theophilus—last iconoclast Emperor.
843	Final restoration of icon worship.
860	Northmen from Russia attack Constantinople. St. Cyril's mission to the Khazars.
863	Defeat of Arabs at Poson.
864	Conversion of Bulgaria.

867–886   Reign of Basil I, founder of the Macedonian dynasty (to 1055).

886–912   Reign of Leo VI—mosaic in narthex of Church of the Holy Wisdom, Constantinople.

893–927   Reign of Simeon in Bulgaria: Simeon's victory at the Achelo river (917).

923–944   Eastern campaigns of John Courcouas.

961   Capture of Crete by Nicephorus Phocas.

963–969   Reign of Nicephorus II (Phocas).

965   Nicephorus II captures Tarsus and Cyprus.

969   Nicephorus II captures Antioch and Aleppo.

969–976   Reign of John I (Tzimisces).

971   Defeat of Northmen from Russia at Silistria.

975   Invasion of Palestine by John I.

976–1025   Reign of Basil II.

989   Baptism of Vladimir of Kiev.

990–1019   Conquest of Bulgaria (Samuel) by Basil II.

995–1022   Basil II's eastern conquests and settlement: annexation of Armenia.

c.1000   The 'Veroli' ivory casket: mosaic decoration of the Church of the Holy Luke in Stiris.

1034–1041 Reign of Michael IV—debasement of gold currency.

1042–1055 Reign of Constantine IX. Mosaic of the Emperor in the Holy Wisdom, Constantinople: other schemes in Nea Mone, Chios and in the Holy Wisdom at Kiev.

1055   Seljuqs occupy Baghdad and enter the service of the Abbasid caliphs.

1071   Romanus IV defeated and captured by Seljuqs under Alp Arslan at Manzikert.

1071–1078 Reign of Michael VII.

1071   Loss of Bari and South Italy to the Normans.

1071–1081 Seljuq conquest of Anatolian highlands.

1081–1118 Reign of Alexius I (Comnenus). Mosaics in the Church at Daphni completed at this time.

1082	Alexius grants large trading concessions to Venice.
1091	Alexius defeats the Patzinaks.
1092	Reform of the coinage by Alexius.
1097	Passage of First Crusade—Jerusalem taken 1098.
1118–1143	Reign of John II, son of Alexius I.
1143–1180	Reign of pro-western Manuel I, son of John II.
1164	Church of St. Pantaleimon at Nerezi founded by a member of the Comnenus family.
1176	Seljuq victory over Manuel at Myriocephalum.
1182	Massacre of Latins in Constantinople.
1183–1185	Reign of Andronicus I—last of the Comnene dynasty.
1184	Isaac Comnenus usurps power in Cyprus.
1185	Thessalonica captured and sacked by Normans.
1185–1204	Dynasty of the Angeli.
1187	Saladin defeats Crusaders at Hattin and captures Jerusalem.
1204	Foundation of the Empire of Trebizond (Comnenus family).
1204	Capture of Constantinople by Fourth Crusaders—Latin Emperors until 1261.
1204–1261	Lascarid dynasty in Nicaea: Theodore crowned 1206. Michael Angelus, Despot of Epirus.
1205	Defeat of Baldwin I by Bulgarians.
1215	Fourth Lateran Council (Innocent III).
1245	First Council of Lyons (Innocent IV).
1259	Accession of Michael VIII (Palaeologus) to throne of Nicaea. Nicaean forces defeat Epirot and Latin army at Pelagonia. Mistra, recently built by Villehardouin, handed over to Byzantines.
1261	Nicaean forces find Constantinople undefended.
1266	Charles of Anjou defeats Manfred of Sicily at Benevento.
1274	Second Council of Lyons called by Gregory X: representatives of Greek Orthodox Church present: personal submission to Rome of Michael VIII.

1275	Michael VIII successful against Latins in naval action at Demetrias.
1280	Charles of Anjou's forces defeated by Greeks at Berat.
1281	Excommunication of Michael VIII by Martin IV (supporting Charles of Anjou).
1282	The Sicilian Vespers—defeat of Charles of Anjou. Death of Michael VIII: accession of his son Andronicus II.
1294	Death of ex-Patriarch John Beccus.
1303	Andronicus uses the Catalan Company as mercenaries.
1308	Ottoman Turks capture Ephesus: Brusa 1326; Nicaea 1329: Nicomedia 1337.
1309	The Popes at Avignon (till 1377).
c. 1320	Completion of mosaic decoration at the Kariye Camii, Constantinople under patronage of Theodore Metochites (c. 1269–1332).
1321–1328	Civil war: Andronicus II v. his grandson Andronicus III.
1331–1355	Stephen Dušan, King of Serbia.
1334	Pope organises naval league against Turks.
1339	Andronicus III sends Barlaam as envoy to the Pope.
1341	Death of Andronicus III and accession of his son John V. Rebellion of John VI (Cantacuzenus).
1341	Civil war: regency for John V, with Serbs v. John VI with Turks. Defeat of John V in 1352. Commune ruling Thessalonica till 1350. Synod on Palamism in Constantinople.
1346	Dušan crowned Emperor of the Serbs and Greeks.
1351	Synod in Constantinople approves Palamism.
1352	John VI in communication with the Pope about a Council.
1354	Turks take Gallipoli. Civil war: John VI v. John V backed by Genoese. John VI abdicates in 1355 becoming a monk. John V undisputed Emperor, makes proposition on Union to the Pope.
1359	Naval League against the Turks.

1365	Turks make Adrianople their capital.
1366	John V goes to Hungary for help against Turks.
1369	John V makes personal submission to Rome.
1373	John V becomes vassal of Murat I. Rebellion of his son Andronicus IV suppressed.
1376–1379	Civil war: rebellion of Andronicus IV against his father John V (supported by Manuel his younger son).
1378–1417	The Great Schism in the West (ended by the Council of Constance). Popes return to Rome.
1379	Restoration of John V with Venetian and Turkish help.
1387	Surrender of Thessalonica to Turks.
1389	Battle of Kossovo: fall of Serbian empire to Turks: accession of Beyazit I.
1390	Usurpation of John VII who ousts his grandfather John V (dies 1391).
1391–1425	Reign of Manuel II.
1393	Turks conquer Thessaly: capture of Trnovo and end of the Bulgarian empire.
1396	Defeat of Crusaders at Nicopolis. Manuel Chrysoloras begins teaching Greek at Florence.
1397–1402	Siege of Constantinople by Beyazit I but Turks defeated by Timurlane at Ankara (1402).
1399–1402	Manuel II tours Europe to find support. Entertained by Henry IV in London, Dec. 1400.
1414–1418	Council of Constance.
1417	Election of Martin V—end of Great Schism. Manuel II builds the Hexamilion but it is easily captured by Murat II (1423).
1421	John VIII becomes co-emperor: sole emperor, on death of Manuel (1425).
1422	Murat II besieges Constantinople.
1423	Thessalonica handed over to Venetians by its Governor.
1428	Restoration of Pantanassa Church at Mistra, with frescoes.
1430	Capture of Thessalonica by Turks.

1431   Council of Basle: Eugenius IV follows Martin V as Pope.

1437   November—Greeks set out for papal Council in Ferrara. Transfer of Council to Florence in 1439—in July, Act of Union of the Churches. Greeks reach Constantinople, Feb. 1440.

1444   Defeat of Hungarians and Crusaders at Varna.

1448   Death of John VIII: accession of his brother Constantine XI: coronation in Mistra 1449.

1451   Mehmet II becomes Sultan.

1452   Union of Churches proclaimed in Constantinople.

1453   May 29th—Constantinople taken by the Turks.

1460   Mistra falls to Turks.

1461   Trebizond falls to Turks.

1481   Death of Mehmet II when preparing expedition against Italy.

1541–1614 El Greco: Crete—Venice—Spain.

1669   Turks capture Crete from Venice.

1683   Turks fail to capture Vienna.

Index

Abbasid caliphate, 88; art in, 151
Acropolites, George, 118–19, 127
administrative system, 3, 6, 13, 21, 22, 29–30, 53–5, 88–9, 126; civil service, 55, 69–70, 79, 87, 89; feudalism, 89–91, 106; *pronoia*, 89
Adrianople, Battle of, 9, 11
Agathius, historian, 19, 43
agriculture, 67, 97
Albert, king of Romans, 131
Aleppo, 65, 77
Alexandria, 12, 42, 57
Alexius I Comnenus, Emperor, 72, 86, 88, 93, 108; Alexiad, 97–101; campaigns, 96, 98–101; coinage, 155, *7b*
al-Ma-'Mun, Caliph, 53
Alp Arslan Seljuq leader, 95
Amalasuntha, Queen of Goths, 20
Amorian dynasty, 56, 77
Anatolia, 88, 91ff., 100; art in, 139, 141–2
Andrew I, King of Hungary, crown, 154, *5a*
Andronicus I Comnenus, Emperor, 108
Andronicus II Palaeologus, Emperor, 118, 121, 122, 124
Andronicus III Palaeologus, Emperor, 122–3, 124
Andronicus IV Palaeologus, Emperor, 125
Angelus dynasty, 85, 106, 107, 109
Angevins, 121
Anna Comnena, historian, 97–102
Anne of Savoy, Empress, 123
Antae, barbarians, 31
Anthemius of Tralles, 19, 24, 147
Antioch, 21, 57, 63, 65, 77
Antioch, Patriarch of, 53, 102
Arabs, 6; culture, 51, 53; pirates, 52; wars with, 42, 44–5, 49, 97, 150
archers, with cataphracts, 74
architecture, 19, 92, 141, 143, 146, 148–9, 158–9, *2b, 7a*
Arian heresy, 11, 20
aristocracy: of Constantinople, 22, 26, 54, 55, 75; feudal, 89, 91; military, 55–56, 66–7, 68–73, 77, 78, 91

Armenia, Armenians, 55, 64ff., 77–8 92ff.; art, 92
army, 57, 79; conscription for, 75; mercenaries in, 89, 90, 95; theme system, 54; *see also* military, *pronoia*
art, 6, 19, 85, 137–43, 145, 155–7, *1–8*; ninth to eleventh centuries, 151–60; twelfth century, 93, 109; iconoclasm and, 139, 150–1; *see also* mosaics, wall paintings
Artzruni, 94; Sennacherib, 95
Asia Minor: art, 139; Christianity in, 12; part of Empire, 65, 66, 113–14; population, 96; wars in, 44, 49, 57, 85, 122–123
Athanasian creed, 11–12
Athens occupied by Grand Company, 122
Attila, Hun, 10–11
Augustine, Saint, 11
Avars, invaders, 30–2, 34, 41, 46

Bagratids, 94
Baldwin, Latin Emperor, 113, 114
Balkans, 52, 65; art, 138, 156; Christianity, 12; invaded, 30–2, 34, 41, 123; rebellion, 86, 93–4, 108–9
banjo, pandiorion, 4
barbarians, 9–11, 12–13, 20–1, 29–35, 55
Bardanes Tourkos, 55, 56
Barisbakourios, 55
Barlaam, Orthodox monk, 124
Basel, Council of, 129
Basil I, Emperor, 64, 67–8
Basil II, Emperor, 5, 64–5, 69, 75, 78–9, 86ff.
Basil Pediaditis, 72
Beccus John, Patriarch, 118, 120, 121
Beirut, 57
Belisarius, 19ff.
Bell, Clive, art historian, 137
Bessarion, Cardinal, 127, 160
Blasius, Saint, of Amorium, 52
Blemmydes Nicephorus, historian, 127
Bohemund, 100, 101, 102
Boniface of Montferrat, 113, 114
Bourbon kings of France, 67

Browne, Edith, art historian, 137
Brutus, L. Junius, 4
Bryennius, Joseph, theologian, 127
Buda Pest, crown of Saint Andrew, *5a*
Bulgaria, Bulgars, 31, 52, 53, 77ff., 126;
    christianity, 77; kingdom of, 44, 109;
    wars with Empire, 50, 63ff., 113–14,
    123
Burgundians, 9
Byron, *Maid of Athens*, 3

Caesarea, 57
Calecas, Michael, historian, 127
Cantacuzeni dynasty, 91
Cappadocia, Greeks in, 96
Cappadocia, John of, 26, 28
Carthage, Exarchate, 29–30, 54
Catalan or Grand Company, 122
cataphracts, 66, 73–4
Cecaumenus, commander, 71–3
Çepni, Turkomans, 97
Chalcedon, Council of, 12, 26
Chalcocondyles, Laonicus, 127
Charlemagne (Karoulos), 53
Charles of Anjou, 117, 121
Chios, Nea Mone, *Anastasis, 1b*
Choniates Nicetas, 103–4, 107–8
Christianity, 7; art, influence on, 142–6,
    150–60; as basis of Empire, 8–9, 57,
    58; decline of, 96, 106–7; iconoclasm,
    44–51, 58, 150–2; Orthodox, 11–13,
    24, 25–6, 77, 93, 96, 103, 109, 124;
    provincial sectarianism, 11–13; schism,
    102, 121, 124, 128–32
Chrysanthus, British, 3
Chrysoloras, Manuel, scholar, 127
Church, 132; and Empire, 66, 103; and
    State, 13, 25–6, 96, 106; negotiations
    for unity, 102, 109, 115–21, 125, 128–
    131
Cimabue, artist, 160
Clement IV, Pope, 117
Codex Justinianus, 23–4
coins, 17, 142, 150, 151, 154–5, *7b*
Comnenus dynasty, 5, 85, 86, 95, 97; art,
    139, 154–6
Conrad III, German Emperor, 105
Constance, Council of, 128
Constans II, Emperor, 43
Constantine I, the Great, Emperor: art,
    140, 145; character, 6, 7; Christianity,
    7–9; founded Constantinople, 7, 63
Constantine V, Emperor, 49; coin, *7b*
Constantine VII, Emperor, ivory, *6b*
Constantine IX, Emperor, 72, 154;
    enamel, *5a*
Constantine XI, Palaeologus, Emperor,
    126

Constantinople: administration, 3, 6, 13;
    attacks on, 10, 114; as capital of East,
    3, 7, 57, 109, 117; culture, 19, 56, 86–7,
    127–8, 142, 147, 159; division of, 113,
    114, 124; fall of, 86, 113, 131–3;
    foundation of, 7; rebuilding after Nika
    riot, 24; religion, 12–13, 124; sack of,
    6, 104–5, 108, 115–16; siege of, 42, 44,
    126, 128, 131–3; University of, 93; *see
    also* Istanbul
Constantinople, Patriarch of, 13, 20, 33,
    114, 118, 120, 127–8; in civil service,
    55, 87, 89; Latin rival, 102, 116
Constantius, Emperor, 6
Cosmas Indicopleustes, sailor, 19, 35
Courcouas, John, Marshal, 64, 75, 77
Crete, 64, 65, 77; art, 160
crusades, 109; First, 95, 100–2; Second,
    96; Third, 94, 96; Fourth, 104–6, 108,
    113; of Nicopolis, 126; under John
    Hunyadi, 131
culture, 19, 56, 57–8, 66; early flowering,
    51; late flowering, 86, 93, 109, 126–7,
    132
currency, 6; debased, 90–1, 154
Cydones, Demetrius, historian, 127
Cyprus, 65
Cyril, Patriarch of Alexandria, 12

Dalton, O. M., art historian, 137
Damascus, 57, 78
Dandolo, Henry, Doge, 108, 113
Danube, frontier of Empire, 29, 30, 32,
    75
Daphni, church art, 152, 153, *2a*; Church
    of the Dormition, *2b*
David Comnenus of Trebizond, 106
Demetrius Cydones, 127
Diehl, Ch., art historian, 137
Diocletian, Emperor, 6, 7; architecture,
    145
Domenicos Theotocopoulos (El Greco),
    160
Dumbarton Oaks Centre of Byzantine
    Studies, 138, 154
Dushan, Stephen, King of Serbia, 123

economy, decline of, 28–9, 90–1, 122,
    149; sound, 152
Egypt, 12, 26, 28, 42, 65
el Greco (Domenicos Theotocopoulos),
    160
Emperors, 3, 6, 11, 85, 150; authority
    over Church and State, 24, 26, 27,
    military, 68–9, 71, 150; difficulties
    with heretics and Popes, 12, 27, 117–
    120, 129–30; Greek and Latin, 113,
    114

Empire, 141–2; Byzantine, 3–7, 33, 41, 117, 122; civil war, 123, 124, 126; collapse, 79, 88, 109; condition of, 51–2, 96, 97, 106, 109; Danube as frontier, 29; division of, 34–5; Latin, 113–16; Roman, 3, 6, 17, 33, 41; travel in, 52; universal Christian, 19, 35, 58, 63–79, 117–20, 129–30; weakness of, 33
enamel cloisonné, 154, *5a*
Ephesus, 52, 57; Councils I and II, 12
Epirus, despotate, 113, 115; architecture, 159
Eugenicus, theologian, 127
Eugenicus, Mark, Metropolitan of Ephesus, 131
Eugenius IV, Pope, 129, 131
Exarchates, Carthage and Ravenna, 29–30, 54

Ferrara, Council of, 129–30
Fetiye Camii, *Pantocrator* mosaic, *8b*
filioque controversy, 117–20, 129–30
Forty-Cubits-High, Jewish leader, 47–8; *see* Iconoclasm
Franks, 9, 10, 34, 99, 100, 101, 103, 104
Frederick I, Barbarossa, 23, 105
Frend, W. H. C., historian, 11

Gainas, Gothic leader, 10
Galla Placidia, mausoleum of, 145
Gaza, 57
Gelimer, Vandal king, 20
Gemistus Pletho (George), historian: art, 157–8; *The Laws*, 127
Gennadius, Patriarch, 127–8
Genoa, trade, 123–4
George Acropolites, 118–19, 127
George Gemistus Pletho, 127, 157–8
George Pachymeres, 120, 127
George Pisidia, 43
George Scholarios, 127–8, 131
George Sphrantzes, 127, 128
Georgians, 78, 96
Gepids, barbarians, 31
Germain, Saint, of Auxerre, shroud, 149
Germanus, Patriarch in 717, 57
Germanus, Patriarch in 1274, 118
Gibbon, Edward, 4, 5, 7
Giotto, painter, 160
Giustiniani, Genoese, 131
Goths, 9, 10, 17, 20–1, 34
Gourgen, *see* Courcouas
Grand Company (Catalan), 122
Greek kingdoms, 113
Gregoras Nicephorus, 127
Gregory II the Great, Pope, Saint, 32–3
Gregory VII, Pope, Saint, 102
Gregory X, Pope, 117–18

Gregory Mammas, Patriarch, 131
Gregory, Bishop of Nyssa, Saint, 8
Gregory Palamas, monk, 124
Gregory the Decapolite, Saint, 52, 140

Harun-ar-Rashid, 51
Hellenism, 109, 142, 146; in art, 151, 152, 157, 160
Henry VI of Germany, Emperor, 105
Henry Dandolo, Doge, 108, 113
Henry of Flanders, Emperor, 114
Heraclian dynasty, 41, 44, 66
Heraclius, Emperor, 5, 33, 41–3, 150, *7b*
Herculaneum, mosaics, 145
heresies, 11–13, 26, 58; Arian, 11, 20; Monophysite, 11, 12, 26, 27, 33; Nestorian, 11, 12; political effects, 12
heretics, 20; Marcellus, 48; Nestorius, 11, 12; treatment of, 26, 27
hexamilion, wall, 126
historians, 6, 12, 17, 19, 28, 43, 67, 73, 105, 127, 137–8
Holy Wisdom, Church of the (St. Sophia), 19, 24–5, 139, 140, 146ff., *3a*, *3b*
Huns, 6, 9, 10–11
Hunyadi, John, crusader, 131

Iconoclasm, 44–51; art under, 139, 142, 150–2; defeat of, 58; origin, 45, 46–8
Indicopleustes, Cosmas, sailor, 19, 35
Innocent III, Pope, 102, 109, 115–16
Innocent IV, Pope, 115, 117
Irene, regent Empress, 50, 53
Irene, wife of Alexius I, 98
Isaac, Bishop of Ephesus, 120
Isaac Comnenus of Cyprus, 106
Isaurian dynasty, 44, 66, 139, 150
Isidore, Cardinal, 131
Isidore of Kiev, theologian, 127
Isidore of Miletus, architect, 19, 24, 147
Islam, 99, 103, 104
Istanbul, art, *3a*, *3b*, *4a*, *4b*, *6a*, *7a*, *8b*
Italy: culture, 126–7; part of Empire, 20, 52, 65, 79; invasions of, 17, 29–30, 34, 42
ivory trade, 142, 149, 153–4, *5b*, *6b*

Jerusalem, 42, 78; Patriarch of, 102
Jews, 26, 46, 47
John I Zimisces, Emperor, 5, 70, 73, 75ff.
John II Comnenus, Emperor, 96, 97, 155, *7b*
John III Ducas, Vatatzes, Emperor, 114–17
John V Paleologus, Emperor, 123, 124, 125

John VI Cantacuzenus, Emperor, 122ff., 127
John VIII Palaeologus, Emperor, 128-9
John Beccus, 118, 120-1
John of Cappadocia, Prefect, 26, 28
John Courcouas, Marshal, 64, 65, 77
John Hunyadi, crusader, 131
John Lydus, 28
John Mauropus, 93
Joseph I, Patriarch of Constantinople, 118, 120, 121
Joseph II, Patriarch of Constantinople, 129, 131
Julian the Apostate, Emperor, 9
Justin I, Emperor, 17
Justin II, Emperor, 29
Justinian I, the Great, Emperor, 16-29; architecture, 19-20, 24-5, 146, 149; art, 19, 145, 146, 7b; Church of Holy Wisdom, 19, 24-5; dissension with Popes, 26-7; Law, 19, 23-4; Nika riot, 19-20; Orthodox Christianity, 12, 24, 25-7; unification of Empire, 17, 20-1, 22, 33-5
Justinian II, Emperor, 44, 54, 7b

Kariye Camii, 147-8, 156-7, 4a, 4b, 6a
Khusro II, Emperor of Persia, 42
Kiev, 65, 67
Krum, Khan of Bulgaria, 50
Kulakovsky, historian, 73

Ladislas, King of Hungary, 131
language, 3, 51, 67, 87, 93, 132
Laonicus Chalcocondyles, 127
Lascaris, Theodore, 117
Lateran Council in 1215, 116
law, 19, 23, 24
Lemerle, Paul, 64
Leo III of Syria, Emperor, 5, 44-5, 48-9, 51; iconoclasm, 49; legal code, 23
Leo V, the Armenian, Emperor, 50, 56
Leo VI, the Wise, Emperor: art, 140, 152; legal code, 23; Taktika, 70
Leo the Deacon, 75-6
Leo the Philosopher, 53
Leo Phocas, commander, 71
Leon Sgouros of W. Morea, 106
Licinius, ruler of East, 6
literature, 7, 11, 19, 41, 51, 86
Liutprand of Cremona, 13
Lombards, invaders, 29-30, 34, 42
London in 1400, 4
Lydus, John, historian, 28
Lyons: 1st Council of, 117; 2nd Council of, 118, 119-20

Macedonia, 123

Macedonian dynasty, 67-8, 78, 85, 87; art, 151-2
Malik Sah, Sultan, 99
Manfred of Sicily, 117
Mankaphas, Theodore, 106
Manuel I, Comnenus, Emperor, 96, 102
Manuel II, Roman Emperor, 4, 125-9
Manuel Chrysoloras, 127
Manzikert, Battle, 65, 85, 86, 91, 95, 96
Marcellus, heretic, 48
Mark Eugenicus, Metropolitan of Ephesus, 131
Martin IV, Pope, 121
Martin V, Pope, 128, 129
Matthew of Edessa, 88, 94-5
Maurice, Emperor, 29, 32, 54
Mauropus, John, theologian, 93
Maxentius, 145
Mehmet II, 126, 131
Mesarites, Nicholas, historian, 105
Metochites, Theodore, Grand Logothete, 127, 158
Metrophanes, Patriarch, 131
Michael II, the Amorian, Emperor, 51, 56
Michael III, Emperor, 77, 150
Michael VII, Ducas, Emperor, 86-7, 88, 95
Michael VIII, Palaeologus, Emperor, 115, 117; campaigns, 115, 122; Council of Lyons, 118-21; culture, 127
Michael IX, Palaeologus, Emperor, 122
Michael III, Patriarch, 103
Michael Calecas, 127
Michael Ducas of Epirus, despot, 114
Michael Psellus, see Psellus
military: administration, 90; aristocracy, 55-6, 68ff., 77-8, 87, 95; caste, 66; tactics, 70-1, 73-5, 76-7
Millet, Gabriel, 137
Mistra, art centre, 157-8, 159
monks, 49, 75, 93, 106-7
mosaics, 93, 140-2, 145, 147-53, 1a, 2a, 3, 4a, 6a, 8b; miniature, 158
Moscow, ivory, 6b
Moslems, 12, 42, 75
Muhammad, 42
Murad II, Sultan, 126

Nacolia, Bishop of, 47-8
Narses, General, 19, 21
navy, 64, 89, 121; league, 124-5
Nerezi, wallpainting, 138, 8a
Nestorius, heretic, 11, 12
Nicaea, 96, 113, 123; art, 151; patriarchate, 113, 116
Nicaea, Council of, 7-8
Nicephorus I, Emperor, 70, 71

Nicephorus II, Phocas, Emperor, 64, 68, 7b; campaigns, 77–8; military treatises, 68–9, 70–1, 73–5
Nicephorus, Patriarch, 51, 55
Nicephorus, Blemmydes, 127
Nicephorus, Gregoras, 127
Nicephorus, Ouranos, Marshal, 73
Nicetas Choniates, 103–4, 107–8
Nicholas Mesarites, 105
Nicomedia, 57, 123
Nika riot, 19–20
Nineveh, Battle of, 42
Normans, 64, 66, 85–6, 100, 104, 108
Notitia Dignitatum, 3
Nymphaeum, Treaty of, 114

Oecumenical Councils: I Nicaea, 7–8; II Constantinople, 164; III Ephesus, 12; IV Chalcedon, 12, 26; V Constantinople, 27; VI 167; VII, 46–8, 50; Florence and Ferrara, 129–30
Okunev, historian, 138
Omur Bey, 125
Ostrogoths, 17
Otto III, German Emperor, 67
Ouranos, Nicephorus, Marshal, 73

Pachymeres, George, 120, 127
pagans, 26, 41
Palaeologus dynasty, 91, 92, 109; art, 126
Palamas, Gregory, monk, 124
Palestine, 12, 42, 45
pandiorion (banjo), 4
Patriarchates, rival, 102
Patzinaks, 100, 102
Paul the Silentiary, 25
Pediaditis, Basil, 72
Pelagonia, Battle of, 115
Peloponnese, 32, 126
Persia: Arab war, 42; religion, 42, 150; Sassanid Empire, 17, 41; wars with Byzantines, 20, 21, 22, 29, 32, 33, 46
Persians, 55
Peter, Tsar of Bulgaria, 77
Pevsner, N. Professor, 145
Philippicus, Emperor, 55
philosophy, 87, 93
Phocas, Emperor, 32, 42
Phocas, Leo, commander, 71
Photius, Patriarch, 51, 55
piracy, 124–5
Pisidia, George, 43
Pitzigaudes, John, 55
plague, 28
Plato, Saint, 55
Pletho, George Gemistus, 127, 157–8
Pompeii, mosaics, 145
Popes: at Avignon, 121; and church

unity, 105, 116–21, 125; and heresies, 26, 27; rival, 128
Procopius of Caesarea, historian, 17–18, 24, 26, 28, 33, 43; *On the Buildings*, 147
pronoia, land tenure, 89, 91, 92
Psellus, Michael, historian, 67, 78–9, 86–7, 88, 89, 91, 93, 95; *Chronographia*, 87

Ravenna: art, mosaics, 145, 148; portraits, 17, 142; Exarchate, 29–30, 54; seat of government, 21, 22, 29; San Apollinaire in Classe, *144*, 147; San Vitale, *144*, 147
religion: art and, 140, 142, 143, 145, 150–60; fanaticism, 5, 71, 74; monasticism, 49, 93; *see also* Christianity
Renaissance, 137, 160; Palaeologan, 156–7, 159
Robert of Courtenay, 114
romaic language, 3
Romanus III, Emperor, 88
Romanus IV Diogenes, Emperor, 95
Romanus Melodus, poet, 19
Rome, 28, 29; art, 143, 145, 146
Russians, war, 75–6

Saborios (Shapur) the Persian, 55
Saladin, captured Jerusalem, 103
Salibas, 55
Salvian of Marseilles, sociologist, 11
Saracens, 63ff, 70, 77, 78
Sassanids, *see* Persia
scholars, 19, 53, 55, 127
Scholarius, George, theologian (Gennadius), 127–8, 131
sculpture, 143
Sennacherib Artzruni, 94
Serbs, 123, 125, 126; art, 156
Sgouros, Leon of W. Morea, 106
Sicilian Vespers, 121
Sicily, 17, 20–2, 65
silk trade, 22–3, 149
Simocatta, Theophylactus, 43
Slavs, 6, 31–2, 33, 41, 52, 55; agriculture, 32; in Anatolia, 96; in Asia Minor, 67
Socrates, historian, 11
Sozomen, historian, 11
Spain, 29
Sphrantzes, George, historian, 127–8
Stephen Dustan, King of Serbia, 123
Stiris, mosaic, *1a*
Süleyman II, Seljuq, 107
Symeon, Tsar of Bulgaria, 70, 75, 77
Symeon the New, Saint, 93
Synesius, Bishop, 10
Syria, Syrians, 42, 55, 88; Monophysite, 12, 26, 28; art, 141

Talbot Rice, David, art, 137
Tarasius, Patriarch, 51, 55
Tarsus, 63, 65, 77
taxation, 28, 106, 122; *allelengyon*, 88;
    army exemption, 68–70
theme-system, 54–5, 57, 92
Theodahad, 20
Theodora, Empress, d.H.D. 548, 12, 18, 27
Theodora, Empress, ninth century, 150
Theodora, Empress, eleventh century,
    67
Theodore I, Lascaris, Emperor, 113–4
Theodore II, Lascaris, Emperor, 117
Theodore Ducas of Epirus, Emperor,
    114
Theodore the Studite, Saint, 48–9, 51, 55
Theodore Mankaphas, 106
Theodore Metochites, 158
Theodore (Poor) Prodromus, 106, 107
Theodosius I, Emperor, 11; art, 142
Theodote, Empress, 55
theologians, theology, 19, 93, 127–8
Theophanes, historian, 49–50, 51, 53
Theophanes, Saint, 55
Theophanes the Greek, 157
Theophilus, Emperor, 51, 53; art, 139
Theophylact, Archbishop, 101, 102
Theophylactus Simocatta, 43
Thessalonica, 57, 104, 108, 113; architec-
    ture, 149, 159; art, 145, 146, 151
Thessalonica, Council of, 117
Thomas the Slav, 53, 56
Thrace, 65, 109
Three Chapters, 27
Tiberius II, Emperor, 29
Timurlane, 126
Totila, Ostrogoth, 21
trade, 64; with far East, 22, 30; ivory,

149; Mediterranean, 41, 108, 123–4;
    silk, 22–3, 149
Trebizond, 65, 96, 113; art, 156
Tribgild, Goth, 10
Tribonian, 19, 26; *Codex Justinianus*, 23
True Cross, 42
Turks, 122, 123, 125–6, 128–9, 131–2;
    art, 160; Ottoman, 6, 92, 109, 126;
    Seljuq conquests, 64, Anatolia, 92–3,
    Armenia, 94–5, Asia Minor, 85–6, 88,
    92–9, 108
Turkic Khazars, 53
Turkomans, 97, 99

Urban II, Pope, 102
Urban IV, Pope, 117
Uspensky Gospels, 51

Vandals, 9, 17, 20
Varangian Guard, 4
Venice, 106, 108, 109, 121; art, 154,
    159–60; trade, 123–4
Veroli casket, 153, *5b*
Vigilius, Pope, 27
Villehardouin, crusader, 104
Visigoths, 17, 21–2, 29
Vladimir of Kiev, 140

wall paintings, 138, *4b, 8a*
Wallachia, rebellion, 109
Weitzmann, Kurt, 138, 152

Yeats, W. B., 137, 160
Yezid, Caliph, iconoclast, 46–8
Yugoslavia, 156, 158

Zachariah of Mytilene, 12
Zoe, Empress, *5a*